Building real life web apps with Angular 18 and Spring Boot

ISBN: 9798343648874

Copyright © 2024 by Haris Tsetsekas

Table of Contents

Introduction 5
1. Project setup 7
2. Product list and details page 13
3. Pagination 19
4. Product filtering 27
5. Cart functionality 33
6. Creating the Spring Boot Web API 39
7. API pagination and frontend-backend integration 45
8. Authentication 51
9. Authorization 67
10. Authentication —Access token refresh/revoke 81
11. Checkout 95
12. Order validation and submission 109
13. Error handling and logging 129
14. User registration 141
15. Cart in local storage 165
16. Admin functionality 171
17. Order processing 193
18. Angular testing – part 1 205
19. Angular testing – part 2 215
20. Spring Boot Web API testing 227

Introduction

This book aims to help readers learn Angular 18 and Spring Boot by developing step-by-step on a real-life project.

Let's see the main requirements for this project: The main purpose of the online store is to present users with a catalog of the products on sale. This catalog will provide the ability to search for text, as well as apply simple filters, such as product category. Users may insert the selected products in the cart and then proceed to checkout and submission of their order.

The web store will also enable administrators to modify the product catalog, by adding / editing / deleting products. Administrators will also be able to view submitted orders.

The web store will be open to anonymous users to browse through the catalog. Users will need to register in order to proceed with their purchase. Admin pages will be available only to authorized users.

In order to avoid unneeded complexity and at the same time highlight the important issues of Angular development, the web app will have a simple design. For instance, only the product name and its short description will be maintained, along with the product photo and price. Furthermore, we will not use a lot of CSS in this book, but Bootstrap will be employed in order to attain a simple but elegant design.

In contrast to the store design, its functionality will be far from rudimentary. It is the aim of the tutorial to use as many important capabilities of the Angular framework as possible. For instance, pagination will be used for the catalog main page and filters will appear as pop-up windows. Communication with the backend API will be authenticated via JSON Web Tokens (JWT). Moreover, routing and validation functionality will be used throughout the project.

On the backend side, the API will follow a REST-like approach, using the Spring REST functionality, with Java Persistence Architecture (JPA) and Hibernate. Also, GraphQL will be introduced.

Last but not least, the code will be accompanied by unit tests, where appropriate. This means that we will not try to reach large code coverage, but we will see targeted and detailed examples for each type of testing.

It should be noted that this is not an introduction to Angular, but a more advanced guide to the development of actual web applications with Angular. In order to be able to follow the course of the implementation, some familiarity with JavaScript or Typescript and Angular as well as Java would be necessary. A good place to start is the introduction to Angular at https://angular.dev/tutorials. So, let's get started with the project setup!

1. Project setup

We will need to have the following software installed in our development workstation:

- JDK v.17 and upper
- Node.js (the latest LTS version)
- Angular 18

After we download and install the latest LTS version of Node.js, we open a new Command Prompt and we install (globally) the latest Angular version:

```
npm install -g @angular/cli
```

Our web application will consist of two separate projects, one for the frontend (the web site developed with Angular) and one for the backend (the REST API developed with Spring Boot). The two parts of the web app (frontend and backend) will run on separate servers, or on separate ports on the same server.

We will use Visual Studio Code for the frontend and IDEA Intellij Community Edition for the backend. Both of them are free to use without any fees.

Let's start with the frontend project. We open a Command Prompt in the main folder, and we enter the following command to create a new Angular project:

```
ng new eshop-frontend --no-standalone
```

This will create the basic structure of the Angular project in a new folder. Select "CSS" for the styling format and "No" to enable Server-Side Rendering (SSR) and Static Site Generation (SSG).

At the backend side, we will create a new Spring Boot project using Spring Intializr (https://start.spring.io/). We opt to use the latest stable edition of Spring (3.3.4 in our case) with Java 17 and Maven.

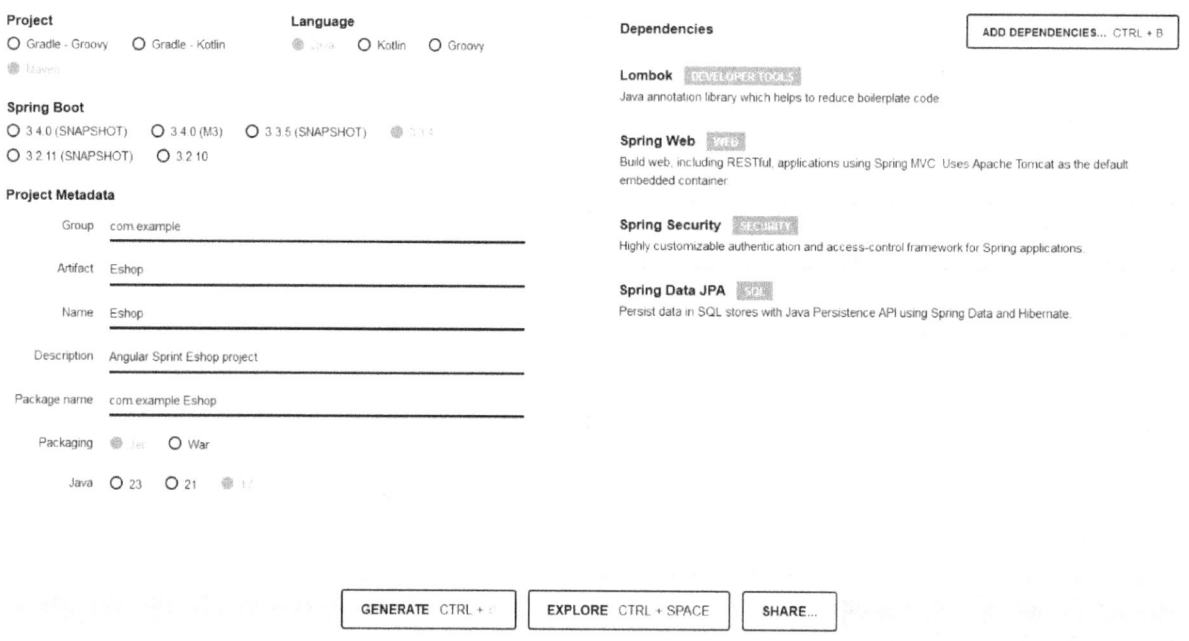

We also choose to add some basic dependencies, like Web, Security, JPA and Lombok. We will add more as we proceed with the development.

When we click on the *Generate* button, we will get a zip file with the generated project. We should unzip in in the main folder and we may also rename the new folder as *eshop-backend*.

We then head to Intellij and we create an new Empty project:

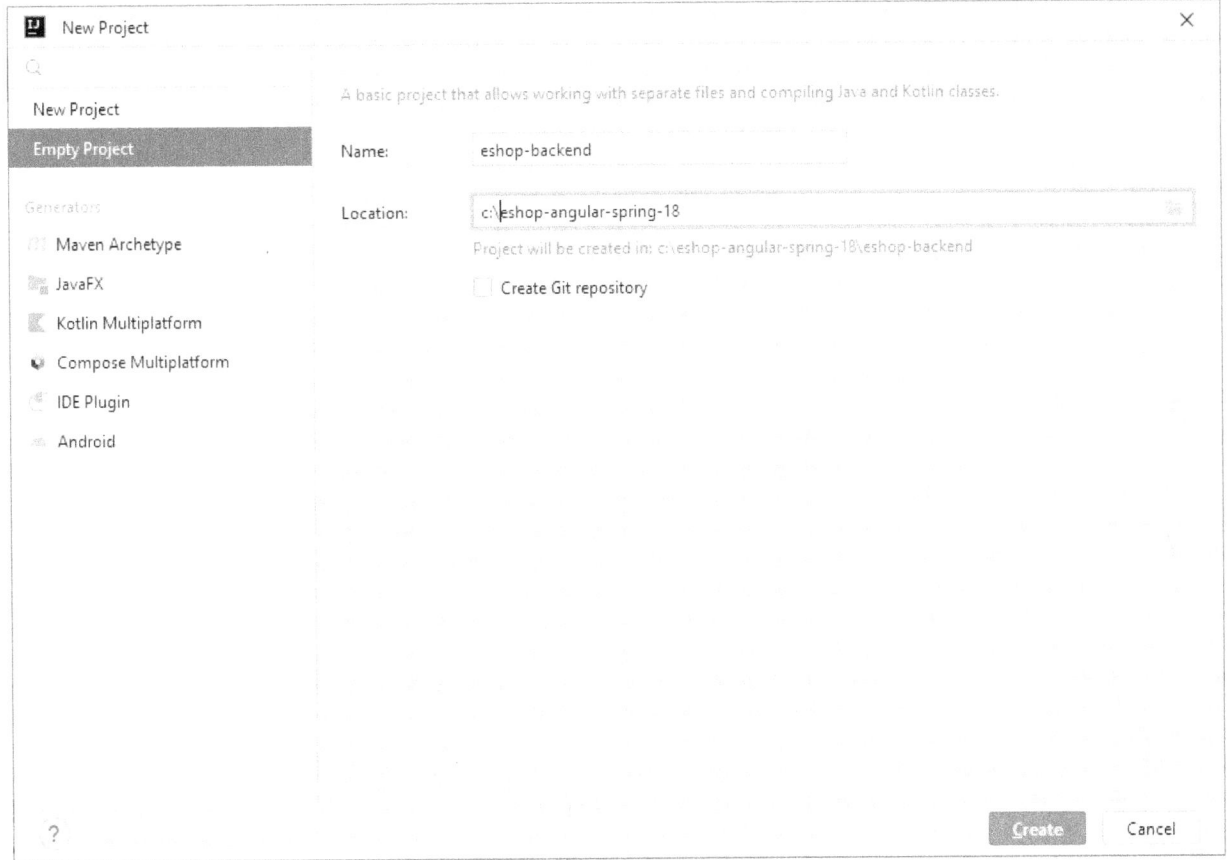

When the project is loaded, Intellij will discover the Maven build scripts and will offer to *Load Maven Project*:

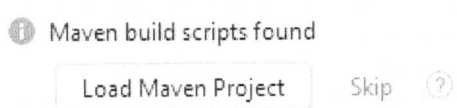

Click on the button and then click on *Recreate* to complete the project initialization.

In the following snippet, we see the pom.xml (Maven's project file) that was generated with this process:

```
<?xml version="1.0" encoding="UTF-8"?>
<project xmlns=http://maven.apache.org/POM/4.0.0
 xmlns:xsi="http://www.w3.org/2001/XMLSchema-instance"
 xsi:schemaLocation="http://maven.apache.org/POM/4.0.0
 https://maven.apache.org/xsd/maven-4.0.0.xsd">
 <modelVersion>4.0.0</modelVersion>
 <parent>
  <groupId>org.springframework.boot</groupId>
  <artifactId>spring-boot-starter-parent</artifactId>
  <version>3.3.4</version>
  <relativePath/> <!-- lookup parent from repository -->
```

```xml
</parent>
<groupId>com.example</groupId>
<artifactId>Eshop</artifactId>
<version>0.0.1-SNAPSHOT</version>
<name>Eshop</name>
<description>Angular Sprint Eshop project</description>
<url/>
<licenses>
 <license/>
</licenses>
<developers>
 <developer/>
</developers>
<scm>
 <connection/>
 <developerConnection/>
 <tag/>
 <url/>
</scm>
<properties>
 <java.version>17</java.version>
</properties>
<dependencies>
 <dependency>
  <groupId>org.springframework.boot</groupId>
  <artifactId>spring-boot-starter-data-jpa</artifactId>
 </dependency>
 <dependency>
  <groupId>org.springframework.boot</groupId>
  <artifactId>spring-boot-starter-security</artifactId>
 </dependency>
 <dependency>
  <groupId>org.springframework.boot</groupId>
  <artifactId>spring-boot-starter-web</artifactId>
 </dependency>

 <dependency>
  <groupId>org.projectlombok</groupId>
  <artifactId>lombok</artifactId>
  <optional>true</optional>
 </dependency>
 <dependency>
  <groupId>org.springframework.boot</groupId>
  <artifactId>spring-boot-starter-test</artifactId>
  <scope>test</scope>
 </dependency>
 <dependency>
  <groupId>org.springframework.security</groupId>
  <artifactId>spring-security-test</artifactId>
  <scope>test</scope>
 </dependency>
</dependencies>

<build>
 <plugins>
```

```xml
<plugin>
 <groupId>org.springframework.boot</groupId>
 <artifactId>spring-boot-maven-plugin</artifactId>
 <configuration>
  <excludes>
   <exclude>
    <groupId>org.projectlombok</groupId>
    <artifactId>lombok</artifactId>
   </exclude>
  </excludes>
 </configuration>
</plugin>
 </plugins>
</build>

</project>
```

LISTING 1-1: pom.xml

Each time we make a change in the *pom.xml* file, we should right-click on this file and select "*Maven->Reload project*" for the changes to take effect. Maven will download the required Java libraries into our project.

Finally, let's try to build our backend project!

Version control

We will use Git for version control. We opt to create a common repository for both projects. Note that Angular initializes by default a Git Repository during the creation of the frontend project. For this reason, we should delete the *.git* folder from inside the frontend folder.

It's better to add only the source and project files in the repository, and to omit compiled (*.class* files in the *target/* folder) and npm packages (in the *node_modules/* folder). Therefore, we may use this minimal .gitignore file in the main folder:

```
target/
node_modules/
```

LISTING 1-2: .gitignore

Next, we open the Command Prompt to the main project folder (the one that contains the two sub-projects). We first create a new repository:

```
git init
```

Next, we proceed with staging all the files:

```
git add .
```

Finally, we commit them in the repository:

```
git commit -m "part1"
```

At the beginning of each chapter, we will create a new git branch (e.g. part2 for chapter 2) where we will create all the new code:

```
git branch part2
git checkout part2
```

Or, in one command:

```
git checkout -b part2
```

At the end of each chapter, after staging and committing the current branch, we will be merging the branch back into the main trunk of the repository:

```
git merge part2
```

If you want to test the code at each chapter, you may checkout the respective branch and open it in the IDEs. For example, the following command:

```
git checkout part2
```

will checkout the code that will have been created by the end of chapter 2.

Now, we are ready to create our first components!

2. Product list and details page

In this chapter, we will create the basic views of our store: the product list and the product details page that will be accessed by customers.

At first, we will use a dummy Angular service to populate both pages. In later iterations of our work, we will introduce data loading from the real API, built with Spring Boot.

Data service

In order to leverage some of the advantages that Typescript brings to web programming, we will introduce typing into the project. For start, we create an interface to describe the item structure:

```typescript
export interface Item {
  id: number;
  name: string;
  price: number;
  category: string;
  description?: string;
}
```

LISTING 2-1: item.ts

The '?' operator in the description parameter means that it is optional and can be left undefined in an *Item* object.

Next, we open either a terminal inside Visual Studio Code or a plain Command Prompt window, and we switch to the frontend project folder. We will create the supporting service (ItemService) by issuing the following command:

```
ng generate service Item
```

This service provides two functions:

- To get the list of all available items
- To get one item only (identified by ID)

Both functions return an Observable. The components that will eventually call those two functions, will have to subscribe to the returned Observables, in order to get their returned items.

```typescript
import { Injectable, } from '@angular/core';
import { Observable, of } from 'rxjs';
import { Item } from './item';

const mock_items = [
  {
    id: 1, name: 'Adidas Stan Smith', price: 90.0,
    category: 'Shoes', description: ''
```

```
  },
  {
    id: 2, name: 'Nike Air Max', price: 110.0,
    category: 'Shoes', description: ''
  },
  {
    id: 3, name: 'Reebok Sweat Shirt', price: 45.0,
    category: 'Clothes', description: ''
  },
  {
    id: 4, name: 'Puma T-Shirt', price: 30.0,
    category: 'Clothes', description: ''
  },
];

@Injectable({
  providedIn: 'root'
})
export class ItemService {

  getItems(): Observable<Item[]> {
    return of(mock_items);
  }

  getItem(id: number): Observable<Item> {
    return of(mock_items[id - 1]);
  }

  constructor() { }
}
```

LISTING 2-2: item.service.ts

Also note that the service defines an array of dummy products that will be used for testing the components.

Product list component

Our first component provides the listing of all available products; this is where all the items for sale are displayed. For the time being, this list will present the full list of available items. In future versions, we will introduce features like product filtering and pagination.

Before all, we should install *ng-bootstrap*, an Angular library based on Bootstrap that will provide formatting options and a lot of useful components for our web app. For Angular 18, Bootstrap 5 is used.

```
ng add @ng-bootstrap/ng-bootstrap
```

Now, to generate the component:

```
ng generate component Items
```

In the new component's template file, an *ngFor iteration displays the available items in a list:

```
<p>Products</p>
<div class="row">
  <div *ngFor="let item of items;" class="col-sm-3">
    <div class="card">
      <div class="card-body">
        <h5 class="card-title">
          <a routerLink="/items/{{item.id}}">{{item.name}}</a>
        </h5>
        <p class="card-subtitle mb-2 text-muted">${{item.price}}</p>
      </div>
    </div>
  </div>
</div>
```

LISTING 2-3: items.component.html

Here, we call the `getItems` function upon initialization and we subscribe to the returned Observable. When the array of items is available, we set the `items` property, that is used by the component template in the *ngFor loop.

```
import { Component, OnInit } from '@angular/core';
import { ItemService } from '../item.service';
import { Item } from '../item';

@Component({
  selector: 'app-items',
  templateUrl: './items.component.html',
  styleUrl: './items.component.css'
})
export class ItemsComponent implements OnInit {

  items: Item[] = [];

  constructor(private itemService: ItemService) { }

  ngOnInit(): void {
    this.getItems();
  }

  getItems(): void {
    this.itemService.getItems()
      .subscribe(items => {
        this.items = items;
      });
  }
}
```

LISTING 2-4: items.component.ts

We add the following router entries inside the *app-routing.module.ts* file, so that the default route and the /items route will both be handled by ItemsComponent.

```
const routes: Routes = [
  {path: '', component: ItemsComponent },
  {path: 'items', component: ItemsComponent }
];
```

LISTING 2-5: app-routing.module.ts

Finally, you may delete the predefined HTML code in *app.component.html* and leave only the <router-outlet> tag at the end of the file. The router outlet is the place where the other components will appear, inside the main page.

```
<router-outlet></router-outlet>
```

Congratulations! You have created you first Angular component. You may give it a try by typing at the command prompt:

```
ng serve
```

This will build our Angular project and will start it on a web server. We may then open this link on our browser:

```
http://localhost:4200
```

Product details

There are two basic options for the display of the product details, when the user clicks on one of the items in the list:

- Display the details in the same page as the list (in a master-detail kind of view) or,
- Route the user to a new page and display the details there.

The second option is more appropriate to the kind of application we are building here. For instance, now the user will be able to bookmark the selected item and open it later for viewing.

We generate the item details component:

```
ng generate component ItemDetails
```

The ItemDetailsComponent class can have the following form:

```
import { Component, OnInit } from '@angular/core';
```

```typescript
import { ActivatedRoute } from '@angular/router';
import { ItemService } from '../item.service';
import { Item } from '../item';

@Component({
  selector: 'app-item-details',
  templateUrl: './item-details.component.html',
  styleUrl: './item-details.component.css'
})
export class ItemDetailsComponent implements OnInit {

  item:Item = { id: 0, name: "", price: 0, category: "", description: "" };

  constructor(
    private route: ActivatedRoute,
    private itemService: ItemService
  ) { }

  ngOnInit(): void {
    this.getItem();
  }

  getItem(): void {
    const id = Number(this.route.snapshot.paramMap.get('id'));
    if (!isNaN(id)) {
      this.itemService.getItem(id)
        .subscribe((item) => {
          this.item = item;
        })
    }
  }
  addToCart(): void { }
}
```

LISTING 2-6: item-details.component.ts

On initialization, we call the `getItem` function of the Item service, while supplying the selected item ID. The ID is conveyed in the URL (e.g. /items/2) and is accessed using a snapshot of the route:

`const id = Number(this.route.snapshot.paramMap.get('id'));`

We should check for the correctness of the ID and the availability of the item. If the ID is wrong, we will display an appropriate message.

Also note that we must initialize the `item` member variable with a dummy value, so that the component template has something to show until the Observable from `getItem` is resolved and updates `item` with the real value.

The template file is more or less straightforward:

```
@if(item){
<h3>{{item.name}}</h3>
```

```html
<div>
  <div class="row">
    <div class="col-md-3"><img src="angular.svg" width="200px"></div>
  </div>
  <div class="row">
    <div class="col-md-3">Description: {{item.description}}</div>
  </div>
  <div class="row">
    <div class="col-md-3">Category: {{item.category}}</div>
  </div>
  <div class="row">
    <div class="col-md-3">Price: {{item.price}}</div>
  </div>
  <div class="row">
    <div class="col-md-3">
      <button (click)="addToCart()" id="addToCart">Add to Cart</button>
    </div>
  </div>
</div>
}
@else {
<div>Product not found!</div>
}
```

LISTING 2-7: item-details.component.html

Finally, let's not forget to update our routing and we are ready to go!

```typescript
const routes: Routes = [
  {path: '', component: ItemsComponent },
  {path: 'items', component: ItemsComponent },
  {path: 'items/:id', component: ItemDetailsComponent }
];
```

LISTING 2-8: app-routing.module.ts

The code repository for this project is available in GitHub:

https://github.com/htset/htset-eshop-angular-18-spring/tree/part2

3. Pagination

Before creating more components and services, it would be advisable to add some structure to the project. We will create dedicated folders for components, services and models. Furthermore, we will add another level inside the components folder, to differentiate between admin and public components, as well as utility components that are shared.

The new project structure is:

```
-components
    -public
    -admin
    -shared
-services
-models
```

We then move the *items* and *item-details* folders into \components\public, as well as *item.ts* file into \models. Moreover, we move the two *item.service.ts* and *item.service.spec.ts* into the \services folder. When we move folders in the VS Code, the IDE offers to update the import paths automatically.

Since there may be thousands of products in the online shop catalog, the items should be retrieved from the API in batches and not all in one go. Every time the user changes page, a new set of items will be retrieved and displayed in the catalog.

The user will also have the option to change the size of the page, i.e. the number of products displayed at the same time. Here too, a change in the page size will result in the retrieval of the appropriate number of items (and a return to the first page).

For this project, the pagination component from Bootstrap will be used (already installed in the second chapter). First of all, a new interface that describes the payload transported from the API is introduced:

```
import { Item } from "./item";

export interface ItemPayload {
  items: Item[];
  count: number;
}
```

LISTING 3-1: itemPayload.ts

Parameter `count` contains the *total* number of items contained in the database and will be used to calculate the number of pages. Parameter `items` contains only the list of items returned after each API call.

Now, we change the dummy `ItemService` in order to use `ItemPayload` objects to provide a subset of `Items` to the component:

```
getItems(page:number, pageSize:number): Observable<ItemPayload> {
  let payload:ItemPayload = {
    items: mock_items.slice((page-1)*pageSize, page*pageSize),
    count: mock_items.length
  }
  return of(payload);
}
```

LISTING 3-2: item.service.ts

In the `ItemsComponent` template, we add the pagination component, as well as a drop-down control for the selection of page size:

```
<p>Products</p>

Page size:
<select [(ngModel)]="storeService.pageSize" id="pageSize">
  <option value="3">3</option>
  <option value="5">5</option>
  <option value="10">10</option>
  <option value="50">50</option>
</select>
<br />

<div class="row">
  <div *ngFor="let item of storeService.items;" class="col-sm-3">
    <div class="card" style="width: 15rem">
      <div class="card-body">
        <h5 class="card-title">
          <a routerLink="/items/{{item.id}}">{{item.name}}</a>
        </h5>
        <p class="card-subtitle mb-2 text-muted">${{item.price}}</p>
      </div>
    </div>
  </div>
</div>

<ngb-pagination [(page)]="storeService.page"
                [pageSize]="storeService.pageSize"
                [collectionSize]="storeService.count"
                (pageChange)="onPageChange($event)">
</ngb-pagination>
```

LISTING 3-3: items.component.html

The `ngb-pagination` component takes the following parameters:

- page: the current page
- pageSize: the selected page size
- collectionSize: the total count of the items
- pageChange: the handler for the page changing event

We need to store the first three parameters in centralized storage so that they will remain available when we leave the catalog page (e.g. to view the details of a product) and then return back to it.

If those variables were stored locally in the component, we would always return to the first page of the catalog and this page would have again the default page size.

For this reason, we will introduce state management functionality in the project. As the web application grows in size and complexity, our life will be easier if we keep state, especially data that is shared between components, in a central store.

There are different approaches with regard to store management. For this project we will follow the simple solution of an Angular service that uses RxJS BehaviorSubject objects to store data and make them available to components.

Another popular option would the NgRx state management library that is based on the Flux/Redux concepts. However, NgRx is a bit complicated and would be more appropriate for large scale projects.

The basic idea behind this approach is to store each shared variable inside its own BehaviorSubject object:

```
import { Injectable } from '@angular/core';
import { BehaviorSubject } from 'rxjs';

@Injectable({
  providedIn: 'root'
})
export class StoreService {

  private readonly _items = new BehaviorSubject<Item[]>([]);
  readonly items$ = this._items.asObservable();

  get items(): Item[] {
    return this._items.getValue();
  }

  set items(val: Item[]) {
    this._items.next(val);
  }

  private readonly _page = new BehaviorSubject<number>(1);
  readonly page$ = this._page.asObservable();

  get page(): number {
    return this._page.getValue();
  }

  set page(val: number) {
    this._page.next(val);
  }

  private readonly _pageSize = new BehaviorSubject<number>(3);
```

```typescript
  public pageSize$ = this._pageSize.asObservable();

  get pageSize(): number {
    return this._pageSize.getValue();
  }

  set pageSize(val: number) {
    this._pageSize.next(val);
  }

  private readonly _count = new BehaviorSubject<number>(1);
  readonly count$ = this._count.asObservable();

  get count(): number {
    return this._count.getValue();
  }

  set count(val: number) {
    this._count.next(val);
  }

  constructor() { }
}
```

LISTING 3-4: store.service.ts

By using the `next()` method of the BehaviorSubject object we can update the value that is stored in it. Moreover, by subscribing to the `page$` or `pageSize$` Observable, a component can be notified about any change in this value.

Also, the `ItemsComponent` class now looks like this:

```typescript
import { Component, OnInit } from '@angular/core';
import { ItemService } from '../../../services/item.service';
import { Item } from '../../../models/item';
import { StoreService } from '../../../services/store.service';

@Component({
  selector: 'app-items',
  templateUrl: './items.component.html',
  styleUrl: './items.component.css'
})
export class ItemsComponent implements OnInit {

  constructor(
    private itemService: ItemService,
    public storeService: StoreService) { }

  ngOnInit(): void {
    this.storeService.pageSizeChanges$
      .subscribe(newPageSize => {
        this.storeService.page = 1;
        this.getItems();
```

```
    });

    this.getItems();
  }

  getItems(): void {
    this.itemService.getItems(this.storeService.page,
      this.storeService.pageSize)
      .subscribe(itemPayload => {
        this.storeService.items = itemPayload.items;
        this.storeService.count = itemPayload.count;
      });
  }
}
```

LISTING 3-5: items.component.ts

Note that we need to add `FormsModule` in the `imports` list in *app.module.ts* file, in order to have `ngModel` directive available in the app module. If we forget it, we will get an error like this one:

`error NG8002: Can't bind to 'ngModel' since it isn't a known property of 'select'.`

The last snippet shows, among others, the use of the `pageSize$` observable. More specifically, we subscribe to this `BehaviorSubject` in order to get notified of any changes in the size of the page.

After playing with the web app, changing pages and viewing products, it seems that pagination does not operate as expected. For example, when the user moves to page 2, views a product and returns to the main page catalog, then the catalog moves to page 1 (and does not remain in page 2 as intended).

The reason lies on the nature of BehaviorSubject: When we subscribe to observable `pageSize$` in `ngOnInit` method, the value stored in the respective BehaviorSubject object is immediately emitted. This results in resetting page variable to 1 as can been seen in the previous snippet.

The solution to this problem is the use of a plain RxJS `Subject` object to store the page size value. `Subject` does not return the current value when being subscribed to and triggers only when function `next` is called.

StoreService looks like this now:

```
import { Injectable } from '@angular/core';
import { BehaviorSubject, Subject } from 'rxjs';
import { Item } from '../models/item';

@Injectable({
  providedIn: 'root'
})
export class StoreService {
```

```typescript
  private readonly _items = new BehaviorSubject<Item[]>([]);
  readonly items$ = this._items.asObservable();

  get items(): Item[] {
    return this._items.getValue();
  }

  set items(val: Item[]) {
    this._items.next(val);
  }

  private readonly _page = new BehaviorSubject<number>(1);
  readonly page$ = this._page.asObservable();

  get page(): number {
    return this._page.getValue();
  }

  set page(val: number) {
    this._page.next(val);
  }

  public pageSize: number = 3;
  public readonly _pageSizeSubject = new Subject<number>();
  public pageSizeChanges$ = this._pageSizeSubject.asObservable();

  private readonly _count = new BehaviorSubject<number>(1);
  readonly count$ = this._count.asObservable();

  get count(): number {
    return this._count.getValue();
  }

  set count(val: number) {
    this._count.next(val);
  }

  constructor() { }
}
```

LISTING 3-6: store.service.ts

The items template has also a modified <select> element:

```html
<select [(ngModel)]="storeService.pageSize"
    (change)="onPageSizeChange()" id="pageSize">
  <option value="3">3</option>
  <option value="5">5</option>
  <option value="10">10</option>
  <option value="50">50</option>
</select>
```

LISTING 3-7: items.component.ts

Also, we modify the ItemsComponent class like this:

```typescript
import { Component, OnInit } from '@angular/core';
import { ItemService } from '../../../services/item.service';
import { StoreService } from '../../../services/store.service';

@Component({
  selector: 'app-items',
  templateUrl: './items.component.html',
  styleUrl: './items.component.css'
})
export class ItemsComponent implements OnInit {

  constructor(
    private itemService: ItemService,
    public storeService: StoreService) { }

  ngOnInit(): void {
    this.storeService.pageSizeChanges$
      .subscribe(newPageSize => {
        this.storeService.page = 1;
        this.getItems();
      });

    this.getItems();
  }

  getItems(): void {
    this.itemService.getItems(this.storeService.page,
      this.storeService.pageSize)
      .subscribe(itemPayload => {
        this.storeService.items = itemPayload.items;
        this.storeService.count = itemPayload.count;
      });
  }

  onPageChange(newPage: number): void {
    this.storeService.page = newPage;
    this.getItems();
  }

  onPageSizeChange(): void {
    this.storeService._pageSizeSubject.next(this.storeService.pageSize);
  }

}
```

LISTING 3-8: items.component.ts

In the above, a handler function (`onPageSizeChange()`)has been added to push the newly selected page size value to the Subject.

The code repository of this part is available in GitHub:

https://github.com/htset/htset-eshop-angular-18-spring/tree/part3

4. Product filtering

In this chapter, we will create a filtering component for the product catalog page. We start by generating the component that implements filtering functionality. This component will be placed in the components/shared folder, as it may be used also in other places.

The FilterComponent class has the following form:

```typescript
import { Component, OnInit } from '@angular/core';
import { Filter } from '../../../models/filter';
import { StoreService } from '../../../services/store.service';
import { NgbActiveModal } from '@ng-bootstrap/ng-bootstrap';

@Component({
  selector: 'app-filter',
  templateUrl: './filter.component.html',
  styleUrls: ['./filter.component.css']
})
export class FilterComponent implements OnInit {
  categories = [
    { name: "Shoes", selected: false },
    { name: "Clothes", selected: false },
    { name: "Gear", selected: false }
  ];

  tempFilter: Filter = { name: "", categories: [] };

  constructor(
    public storeService: StoreService,
    public activeModal: NgbActiveModal
  ) { }

  ngOnInit(): void {
    this.tempFilter = this.storeService.filter;
    this.categories = this.categories
      .map(cat =>
      ({
        name: cat.name,
        selected: (this.tempFilter.categories.includes(cat.name))
      }));
  }

  onChange(): void {
    this.tempFilter.categories = this.categories
      .filter(c => c.selected)
      .map(cc => cc.name);
  }

  onFilterChanged(): void {
    this.storeService.filter = this.tempFilter;
  }
}
```

LISTING 4-1: filter.component.ts

This class uses the definition of Filter interface:

```
export interface Filter{
    name: string;
    categories:string[];
}
```

LISTING 4-2: filter.ts

Also, the actively used filter is stored centrally inside StoreService:

```
...
private   readonly   _filter   =   new   BehaviorSubject<Filter>({name:     "",
categories:[]});
readonly filter$ = this._filter.asObservable();

get filter(): Filter {
  return this._filter.getValue();
}

set filter(val: Filter) {
  this._filter.next(val);
}
...
```

LISTING 4-3: store.service.ts

Finally, the template file for the FilterComponent class is depicted below:

```html
<div class="modal-header">
  <h4 class="modal-title">Products Filtering</h4>
  <button type="button" class="close"
          (click)="activeModal.dismiss()">x</button>
</div>

<div class="modal-body">
  <strong>By text:</strong>
  <input type="text" #searchBox id="searchbox"
    [(ngModel)]="tempFilter.name" /><br />
  <strong>By category:</strong>
  <ul>
    <li *ngFor="let cat of categories" style="list-style-type:none;">
      <input type="checkbox" [(ngModel)]="cat.selected"
             id={{cat.name}} (change)="onChange()" />
      {{cat.name}}
    </li>
  </ul>
</div>
```

```html
<div class="modal-footer">
  <button type="button" id="update" class="btn btn-outline-dark"
          (click)="onFilterChanged()">Update Filter</button>
  <button type="button" class="btn btn-outline-dark"
          (click)="activeModal.close()">Close</button>
</div>
```

LISTING 4-4: filter.component.html

The filter component will appear in a modal window when the user clicks on the *filters* button in the product list. For this reason, `FilterComponent` injects ng-bootstrap's `NgbActiveModal` class, in order to be able to `close()` or `dismiss()` the modal window from within.

The modal window will be opened from a button in the product catalog:

```html
<button (click)="openFilter()">Filters</button>
```

LISTING 4-5: items.component.html

The ItemsComponent class will now have the following form:

```typescript
import { Component, OnInit } from '@angular/core';
import { ItemService } from '../../../services/item.service';
import { StoreService } from '../../../services/store.service';
import { NgbModal } from '@ng-bootstrap/ng-bootstrap';
import { skip } from 'rxjs';
import { FilterComponent } from '../../shared/filter/filter.component';

@Component({
  selector: 'app-items',
  templateUrl: './items.component.html',
  styleUrl: './items.component.css'
})
export class ItemsComponent implements OnInit {

  constructor(
    private itemService: ItemService,
    public storeService: StoreService,
    private modalService: NgbModal) { }

  ngOnInit(): void {
    this.storeService.pageSizeChanges$
      .subscribe(newPageSize => {
        this.storeService.page = 1;
        this.getItems();
      });

    this.storeService.filter$
      .pipe(skip(1))    //skip getting filter at component creation
      .subscribe(filter => {
```

```
        this.storeService.page = 1;
        this.getItems();
      });

    this.getItems();
  }

  getItems(): void {
    this.itemService.getItems(this.storeService.page,
      this.storeService.pageSize,
      this.storeService.filter)
      .subscribe(itemPayload => {
        this.storeService.items = itemPayload.items;
        this.storeService.count = itemPayload.count;
      });
  }

  onPageChange(newPage: number): void {
    this.storeService.page = newPage;
    this.getItems();
  }

  onPageSizeChange(): void {
    this.storeService._pageSizeSubject.next(this.storeService.pageSize);
  }

  openFilter(): void {
    this.modalService.open(FilterComponent);
  }
}
```

LISTING 4-6: items.component.ts

ItemsComponent injects ng-bootstrap's `ModalService` to be able to open a modal window inside the product catalog. Furthermore, the component subscribes to the `filter$` Observable from `StoreService`, so that it will be notified of any change in the filter contents by the user. Note that the component skips getting the filter on the first time it loads to avoid returning to the first page.

Finally, `ItemService` is updated to provide for the filtering of the (still dummy) items:

```
import { Injectable, } from '@angular/core';
import { Observable, of } from 'rxjs';
import { Item } from '../models/item';
import { ItemPayload } from '../models/itemPayload';
import { Filter } from '../models/filter';

const mock_items: ItemPayload = {
  items: [
    {
      id: 1, name: 'Adidas Stan Smith',
      price: 90.0, category: 'Shoes', description: ''
```

```
  },
  {
    id: 2, name: 'Nike Air Max',
    price: 110.0, category: 'Shoes', description: ''
  },
  {
    id: 3, name: 'Reebok Sweat Shirt',
    price: 45.0, category: 'Clothes', description: ''
  },
  {
    id: 4, name: 'Puma T-Shirt',
    price: 30.0, category: 'Clothes', description: ''
  },
  {
    id: 5, name: 'Under Armour',
    price: 130.0, category: 'Shoes', description: ''
  },
  {
    id: 6, name: 'Nike Sweat shirt',
    price: 65.0, category: 'Clothes', description: ''
  },
  {
    id: 7, name: 'Spalding basketball',
    price: 43.0, category: 'Gear', description: ''
  },
  {
    id: 8, name: 'Dumbbell 5kg',
    price: 3.50, category: 'Gear', description: ''
  },
  {
    id: 9, name: 'New Balance',
    price: 120.0, category: 'Shoes', description: ''
  }
  ],
  count: 8
};

@Injectable({
  providedIn: 'root'
})
export class ItemService {

  getItems(page: number, pageSize: number, filter: Filter):
    Observable<ItemPayload> {
    let filteredItems: Item[] = mock_items.items.filter(item => {
      return (
        item.name.indexOf(filter.name) >= 0
        &&
        (filter.categories.length == 0
          || filter.categories.includes(item.category))
      );
    }
    );

    let payload: ItemPayload = {
```

```
    items: filteredItems.slice((page - 1) * pageSize, page * pageSize),
    count: filteredItems.length
  }
  return of(payload);
}

getItem(id: number): Observable<Item> {
  return of(mock_items.items[id - 1]);
}

constructor() { }
}
```

LISTING 4-7: item.service.ts

The code repository of this chapter is available in GitHub:

https://github.com/htset/htset-eshop-angular-18-spring/tree/part4

5. Cart functionality

On this chapter of the online shop tutorial, we will create the Cart component. We start by defining the types for the cart and the items it contains.

The structure of the cart items is defined in `models/cartItem.ts`:

```typescript
import { Item } from "./item";

export class CartItem {
  public item: Item = {
    id: 0, name: "", price: 0,
    category: "", description: ""
  };
  public quantity: number = 0;
}
```

LISTING 5-1: cartItem.ts

Next, `models/cart.ts` implements the functionality of the cart. Note that when the user adds to the cart, a product that is already there, its quantity is increased accordingly.

```typescript
import { CartItem } from "./cartItem";

export class Cart {
  cartItems: CartItem[] = [];

  addItem(cartItem: CartItem) {
    let found: boolean = false;
    this.cartItems = this.cartItems.map(ci => {
      if (ci.item?.id == cartItem.item?.id) {
        ci.quantity++;
        found = true;
      }
      return ci;
    });

    if (!found) {
      this.cartItems.push(cartItem);
    }
  }

  removeItem(item: CartItem) {
    const index = this.cartItems.indexOf(item, 0);
    if (index > -1) {
      this.cartItems.splice(index, 1);
    }
  }

  emptyCart() {
    this.cartItems = [];
  }
```

```
  getTotalValue(): number {
    let sum = this.cartItems.reduce(
      (a, b) => { a = a + b.item?.price * b.quantity; return a; }, 0);
    return sum;
  }

  isCartValid(): boolean {
    if (this.cartItems
      .find(cartitem =>
        (cartitem.quantity == null || cartitem.quantity <= 0)) === undefined)
      return true;
    return false;
  }
}
```

LISTING 5-2: cart.ts

Next, we proceed with generating the cart component:

`ng generate component cart`

This component will depict a list of all products included in the cart, along with their quantities and prices. The user will be able to change the quantity of an item or remove it altogether from the cart. The cart will also present the total amount for payment, as well as options to empty the cart or proceed to checkout.

The cart component template has the following form:

```
<h3>Cart Details</h3>
<table class="table table-striped">
  <tr>
    <th> </th>
    <th>Name</th>
    <th>Unit Price</th>
    <th>Quantity</th>
    <th>Total Price</th>
    <th> </th>
  </tr>
  <tr *ngFor="let item of storeService.cart.cartItems">
    <td>
      <a routerLink="/items/{{item.item.id}}">
        <img src="angular.svg" width="70px" />
      </a>
    </td>
    <td>
      <a routerLink="/items/{{item.item.id}}">
        {{item.item.name}}
      </a>
    </td>
    <td>
      <a routerLink="/items/{{item.item.id}}">
        {{item.item.price}}
```

```html
      </a>
    </td>
    <td>
      <input type="number" [(ngModel)]="item.quantity"
             size="2" id="quantity" />
    </td>
    <td>
      <a routerLink="/items/{{item.item.id}}">
        {{item.item.price * item.quantity}}
      </a>
    </td>
    <td>
      <input type="button" (click)="removeFromCart(item)"
             id="remove" value="Remove" />
    </td>
  </tr>
  <tr>
    <td colspan="4"> </td>
    <td>{{storeService.cart.getTotalValue()}}</td>
    <td> </td>
  </tr>
</table>
<br />
<br />
<button (click)="emptyCart()" id="empty"
        [disabled]="storeService.cart.cartItems.length == 0">
  Empty Cart
</button>
<br />
<br />
<button routerLink="/checkout" id="checkout"
        [disabled]="storeService.cart.cartItems.length == 0
            || !storeService.cart.isCartValid()">
  Go to Checkout..
</button>
<br />
<br />
<button routerLink="">Back to items</button>
<br />
```

LISTING 5-3: cart.component.html

The CartComponent class contains functions for removing one or all items from the cart:

```typescript
import { Component, OnInit } from "@angular/core";
import { CartItem } from "../../../models/cartItem";
import { StoreService } from "../../../services/store.service";

@Component({
  selector: 'app-cart',
  templateUrl: './cart.component.html',
  styleUrls: ['./cart.component.css']
})
```

```
export class CartComponent implements OnInit {

  constructor(public storeService: StoreService) { }

  removeFromCart(item: CartItem){
    this.storeService.cart.removeItem(item);
  }

  emptyCart(){
    this.storeService.cart.emptyCart();
  }

  ngOnInit(): void {
  }

}
```

LISTING 5-4: **cart.component.ts**

The state information about the cart (cart variable) is stored inside `StoreService` with the use of a `BehaviorSubject` object:

```
...
  private readonly _cart = new BehaviorSubject<Cart>(new Cart());
  readonly cart$ = this._cart.asObservable();

  get cart(): Cart {
    return this._cart.getValue();
  }

  set cart(val: Cart) {
    this._cart.next(val);
  }
...
```

LISTING 5-5: **store.service.ts**

Users may add a product in the cart, by pressing the *Add to cart* button in the item details component:

```
...
export class ItemDetailsComponent implements OnInit {

  item:Item = {id:0, name:"", price:0, category:"", description:""};

  constructor(
    private route: ActivatedRoute,
    private itemService: ItemService,
    private storeService: StoreService,
    private router: Router
  ) { }
```

```
...
  addToCart(): void {
    this.storeService.cart.addItem({item: this.item, quantity: 1});
    this.router.navigate(['/cart']);
  }

}
```

LISTING 5-6: item-details.component.ts

In order to be able to navigate to the cart page, the respective route entry should be added in app-routing.module.ts:

```
const routes: Routes = [
  {path: '', component: ItemsComponent },
  {path: 'items', component: ItemsComponent },
  {path: 'items/:id', component: ItemDetailsComponent } ,
  {path: 'cart', component: CartComponent}
];
```

LISTING 5-7: app-routing.module.ts

Finally, we may add a link to the cart page in AppComponent so that users will be able to navigate to the cart from any page:

```
<div *ngIf="storeService.cart.cartItems.length > 0" align="right">
    <a routerLink='cart'>Cart</a>
</div>
<router-outlet></router-outlet>
```

LISTING 5-8: app.component.html

Finally, we should declare StoreService in the constructor of the AppComponent class:

```
import { Component } from '@angular/core';
import { StoreService } from './services/store.service';

@Component({
  selector: 'app-root',
  templateUrl: './app.component.html',
  styleUrls: ['./app.component.css']
})
export class AppComponent {
  title = 'my-eshop';

  constructor(
    public storeService: StoreService
  ) { }
```

}

LISTING 5-9: app.component.ts

Note that the cart needs more functionality, mainly with regard to error handling and input processing. For instance, the cart component should check that the quantity is an integer and inform the user accordingly. Such issues have been left out for simplicity reasons and will be dealt with in a later chapter, where an overall solution for error handling will be presented.

The code repository of this part is available in GitHub:

https://github.com/htset/htset-eshop-angular-18-spring/tree/part5

6. Creating the Spring Boot Web API

So far, our Angular frontend has used a dummy API for displaying products. Now, it is time to use a real API, so we will develop the Spring Boot Web API we created in the first chapter of this book.

We will need to use a database to store our data. Any recent version of MySQL will do just fine, but you can use any other database, like Postgres or MariaDB.

First of all, we will create a structure of the Java packages, so that we can separate the controllers, the services, the models and the other types of classes in our project:

-com.example.Eshop

    -config

    -controllers

    -dtos

    -exceptions

    -models

    -repositories

    -services

Next, we create a model for the eshop items. Inside the `models` package, we add the definition of the `Item` entity that will be used to describe the structure of the Items database table.

```java
package com.example.Eshop.models;

import jakarta.persistence.*;
import lombok.Data;
import java.math.BigDecimal;

@Entity
@Data
public class Item {
  @Id
  @GeneratedValue(strategy = GenerationType.IDENTITY)
  private Long id;
  private String name;
  private BigDecimal price;
  private String category;
  private String description;
}
```

LISTING 6-1: Item.java

We use the `Data` annotation from Lombok to automatically create consrtuctors and getter/setter methods.

DTOs

Next, we add the `ItemPayloadDTO` class that will describe the structure of the JSON data that will be transmitted to the API client:

```java
package com.example.Eshop.dtos;

import com.example.Eshop.models.Item;
import lombok.Data;

import java.util.List;

@Data
public class ItemPayloadDTO {
  private List<Item> items;
  private long count;

  public ItemPayloadDTO(List<Item> items, long count) {
    this.items = items;
    this.count = count;
  }
}
```

LISTING 6-2: ItemPayloadDTO.java

In order to be able to store objects of `Item` class in the database, we need a Repository:

```java
package com.example.Eshop.repositories;

import com.example.Eshop.models.Item;
import org.springframework.data.jpa.repository.JpaRepository;

public interface ItemRepository extends JpaRepository<Item, Long> {
}
```

LISTING 6-3: ItemRepository.java

Next, we provide the database connection details in the *application.properties* file:

```
spring.application.name=Eshop
spring.datasource.url=jdbc:mysql://localhost:3306/eshop_spring_angular?useSSL=false
&allowPublicKeyRetrieval=true
spring.datasource.username=user1
spring.datasource.password=pass1
spring.jpa.hibernate.ddl-auto=update
spring.jpa.properties.hibernate.dialect=org.hibernate.dialect.MySQL8Dialect
```

LISTING 6-4: application.properties

Upon the startup of our application, Hibernate will automatically create the *Item* table in our database. Make sure to connect to MySQL (e.g. with MySQL Workbench) and create the *eshop_spring_angular* database referred to in the *application.properties* file.

Moreover, we should add a MySQL connector dependency in pom.xml:

```xml
<dependency>
  <groupId>mysql</groupId>
  <artifactId>mysql-connector-java</artifactId>
  <version>8.0.33</version>
</dependency>
```

LISTING 6-5: pom.xml

For the next few chapters only, we will disable Spring Security, in order to test the API without further complexity:

```xml
<!--dependency>
  <groupId>org.springframework.boot</groupId>
  <artifactId>spring-boot-starter-security</artifactId>
</dependency-->
```

LISTING 6-6: pom.xml

Reload the Maven project for the change to take effect.

You may also run the following script in the SQL Management Studio to add some items in the database:

```sql
INSERT INTO Item(Name, Price, Category, Description)
    VALUES
        ('Adidas Stan Smith', 90.0, 'Shoes', ''),
        ('Nike Air Max', 110.0, 'Shoes', ''),
        ('Reebok Sweat Shirt', 45.0, 'Clothes', ''),
        ('Puma T-Shirt', 30.0, 'Clothes', ''),
        ('Under Armour', 130.0, 'Shoes', ''),
        ('Nike Sweat shirt', 65.0, 'Clothes', ''),
        ('Spalding basketball', 43.0, 'Gear', ''),
        ('Dumbbell 5kg', 3.50, 'Gear', ''),
        ('New Balance', 120.0, 'Shoes', '')
```

LISTING 6-7: SQL command

Now, we proceed with adding the Items controller class to the project. For the time being, it will serve only requests for one (e.g. GET /items/5) or all items (GET /items) in the database.

The Item controller has the following form:

```java
package com.example.Eshop.controllers;

import com.example.Eshop.dtos.ItemPayloadDTO;
import com.example.Eshop.models.Item;
import com.example.Eshop.services.ItemService;
import com.example.Eshop.exceptions.ItemNotFoundException;
import org.springframework.http.HttpStatus;
import org.springframework.http.ResponseEntity;
import org.springframework.web.bind.annotation.*;
import org.slf4j.Logger;
import org.slf4j.LoggerFactory;

@RestController
@RequestMapping("/items")
public class ItemController {

  private ItemService itemService;
  private final Logger logger = LoggerFactory.getLogger(ItemController.class);

  public ItemController(ItemService itemService){
    this.itemService = itemService;
  }

  @GetMapping
  public ResponseEntity<ItemPayloadDTO> getItems() {
    try {
      ItemPayloadDTO itemPayload = itemService.getItems();
      return  ResponseEntity.ok(itemPayload);  //Return  200  OK  with  the  item payload
    } catch (Exception e) {
      logger.error("Error fetching items: {}", e.getMessage());
      return ResponseEntity.status(HttpStatus.INTERNAL_SERVER_ERROR)
          .body(null); //Return 500 Internal Server Error
    }
  }

  @GetMapping("/{id}")
  public ResponseEntity<Item> getItemById(@PathVariable Long id) {
    try {
      Item item = itemService.getItemById(id);
      return ResponseEntity.ok(item); //Return 200 OK with the item
    } catch (ItemNotFoundException e) {
      logger.error("Item not found with id {}: {}", id, e.getMessage());
      return ResponseEntity.status(HttpStatus.NOT_FOUND)
          .body(null); //Return 404 Not Found if the item is not found
    } catch (Exception e) {
      logger.error("Error fetching item by id {}: {}", id, e.getMessage());
      return ResponseEntity.status(HttpStatus.INTERNAL_SERVER_ERROR)
          .body(null); //Return 500 Internal Server Error for other issues
    }
  }
}
```

LISTING 6-8: ItemController.java

This is a very simple implementation of the controller as there are no options for pagination, filtering and sorting that would be necessary to our frontend. In the next chapter, this functionality will be included in the controller and the API will be made available to the Angular frontend.

When the requested item is not found in the database, then the controller responds with a *404 Not Found* response. If any other error occurs then it responds with *500 Internal Server Error*.

Note that we have added a new exception class to express the absence of an item:

```
package com.example.Eshop.exceptions;

public class ItemNotFoundException extends RuntimeException {

  public ItemNotFoundException(String message) {
    super(message);
  }

  public ItemNotFoundException(String message, Throwable cause) {
    super(message, cause);
  }
}
```

LISTING 6-9: ItemNotFoundException.java

The controller makes use of a service class, that implements the business logic:

```
package com.example.Eshop.services;

import com.example.Eshop.dtos.ItemPayloadDTO;
import com.example.Eshop.exceptions.ItemNotFoundException;
import com.example.Eshop.models.Item;
import com.example.Eshop.repositories.ItemRepository;
import org.springframework.stereotype.Service;
import org.slf4j.Logger;
import org.slf4j.LoggerFactory;

import java.util.List;

@Service
public class ItemService {

  private final ItemRepository itemRepository;
  private static final Logger logger
    = LoggerFactory.getLogger(ItemService.class);

  public ItemService(ItemRepository itemRepository){
    this.itemRepository = itemRepository;
```

```java
    }

    //Get all items
    public ItemPayloadDTO getItems() {
      try{
        List<Item> items = itemRepository.findAll();
        return new ItemPayloadDTO(items, items.size());
      } catch (Exception e) {
        logger.error("Error fetching items: {}", e.getMessage());
        throw new RuntimeException("Unable to fetch items, please try again later");
      }
    }

    //Get one item by ID
    public Item getItemById(Long id) {
      try {
        return itemRepository.findById(id)
            .orElseThrow(()
                -> new ItemNotFoundException("Item not found with id: " + id));
      } catch (ItemNotFoundException e) {
        logger.error("Error fetching item by id {}: {}", id, e.getMessage());
        throw e;
      } catch (Exception e) {
        logger.error("Error fetching item by id {}: {}", id, e.getMessage());
        throw new RuntimeException("Unable to fetch item, please try again later");
      }
    }
}
```

LISTING 6-10: ItemService.java

Now we can run the solution by running the main class (*EshopApplication.java*). To see the backend and get the list of all items that we inserted in the database, we should go to:

`http://localhost:8080/items`

To get the item with ID=1, we should use the following URL:

`http://localhost:8080/items/1`

The resulting project can be found in Github:

https://github.com/htset/htset-eshop-angular-18-spring/tree/part6

7. API pagination and frontend-backend integration

In this chapter we will continue developing the Spring Boot Web API by introducing pagination and integration with the Angular frontend.

API Pagination

The API, as it stands now, needs pagination so that a request to /items will not return the whole inventory of products. The API will have options, not only for pagination, but also for product filtering, based on the name and the category of the product. The GET request to /items will have the following format:

/items?pageNumber=1&pageSize=10&name=Adidas&category=shoes,clothes

In particular, the category parameter will have all requested categories concatenated with the use of the comma (,) symbol.

Let's start with the `ItemController` class and modify the `GetItems` method, so that it can process the query string and filter the products based on the user's request:

```java
...
  @GetMapping
  public ResponseEntity<ItemPayloadDTO> getItems(
      @RequestParam(defaultValue = "0") int pageNumber,
      @RequestParam(defaultValue = "10") int pageSize,
      @RequestParam(required = false) String category,
      @RequestParam(required = false) String name) {
    try {
      //Validate pageNumber and pageSize
      if (pageNumber < 1 || pageSize < 1) {
        return ResponseEntity.badRequest()
            .body(null); //Return 400 Bad Request for invalid page parameters
      }

      ItemPayloadDTO itemPayload = itemService
          .getItems(pageNumber, pageSize, category, name);
      return ResponseEntity.ok(itemPayload); //Return 200 OK with the item payload
    } catch (Exception e) {
      logger.error("Error fetching items: {}", e.getMessage());
      return ResponseEntity.status(HttpStatus.INTERNAL_SERVER_ERROR)
          .body(null); //Return 500 Internal Server Error
    }
  }
...
```

LISTING 7-1: ItemController.java

We also update the ItemService class to handle the query parameters:

...

```java
    //Get items based on pagination
    public ItemPayloadDTO getItems(int page, int size, String category, String name)
    {
      try {
        if (page < 1 || size < 1) {
          throw new
              IllegalArgumentException("Page and size must be greater than 0");
        }

        //Split category string into individual categories
        List<String> categories = Arrays.asList(category.split(","));

        Page<Item> itemPage;
        page -= 1; //Pagination starts with 0, in the frontend we start with 1

        if ((category != null && !category.isEmpty())
            || (name != null && !name.isEmpty())) {
          //If search criteria is provided
          itemPage = itemRepository
              .findByColumnContainingValuesAndFilter(categories,
                  name, PageRequest.of(page, size));
        } else {
          itemPage = itemRepository.findAll(PageRequest.of(page, size));
        }
        return new
            ItemPayloadDTO(itemPage.getContent(), itemPage.getTotalElements());
      } catch (Exception e) {
        logger.error("Error fetching items: {}", e.getMessage());
        throw new RuntimeException("Unable to fetch items, please try again later");
      }
    }
...
```

LISTING 7-2: ItemService.java

We also have to update the repository class, so that a new method is available to the service:

findByCategoryContainingAndNameContaining()

```java
package com.example.Eshop.repositories;

import com.example.Eshop.models.Item;
import org.springframework.data.domain.Page;
import org.springframework.data.domain.Pageable;
import org.springframework.data.jpa.repository.JpaRepository;
import org.springframework.data.jpa.repository.Query;
import org.springframework.data.repository.query.Param;

import java.util.List;
```

```java
public interface ItemRepository extends JpaRepository<Item, Long> {
    @Query("SELECT i FROM Item i " +
        "WHERE (i.category IN :categories) " +
        "AND (i.name LIKE %:name%)")
    Page<Item> findByColumnContainingValuesAndFilter(
        @Param("categories") List<String> categories,
        @Param("name") String name,
        Pageable pageable);
}
```

LISTING 7-3: ItemRepository.java

Now, our controller is ready to process the complex query string listed above.

Integration with frontend

Next, it is time to modify our Angular frontend, so that it can make use of the new API. Both projects will run on the same server (localhost) but on different ports. The frontend runs on port 4200 by default, while the API runs on port 8080.

First of all, since the frontend and the API technically run on different servers, we need to use *CORS (Cross-Origin Resource Sharing)*, so that browsers will allow this communication to take place.

We can configure CORS globally by defining a `CorsConfigurationSource` bean in our `SecurityConfig` class. This ensures that all incoming requests follow the CORS policy across the entire application.

For RESTful APIs, enabling CORS in the security configuration (`SecurityConfig`) is the most common approach, as it provides centralized control. This ensures that our API is accessible to clients (e.g., Angular frontends) running on different origins, like http://localhost:4200.

```java
package com.example.Eshop.config;

import org.springframework.security.config.annotation.web.configuration.EnableWebSecurity;
import org.springframework.context.annotation.Bean;
import org.springframework.context.annotation.Configuration;
import org.springframework.security.config.annotation.web.builders.HttpSecurity;
import org.springframework.security.web.SecurityFilterChain;
import org.springframework.web.cors.CorsConfiguration;
import org.springframework.web.cors.UrlBasedCorsConfigurationSource;
import java.util.List;

@Configuration
@EnableWebSecurity
public class SecurityConfig {

    @Bean
    public SecurityFilterChain securityFilterChain(HttpSecurity http)
```

```java
        throws Exception {
    http
        //Disable CSRF since this is a stateless REST API
        .csrf(csrf -> csrf.disable())
        //Enable CORS
        .cors(cors -> cors.configurationSource(corsConfigurationSource()))
        //Access all endpoints without authentication - for now
        .authorizeHttpRequests(auth -> auth
                .anyRequest().permitAll()
        );
    return http.build();
}

@Bean
public UrlBasedCorsConfigurationSource corsConfigurationSource() {
    CorsConfiguration config = new CorsConfiguration();
    //Allowed origins
    config.setAllowedOrigins(List.of("http://localhost:4200"));
    //Allowed HTTP methods
    config.setAllowedMethods(List.of("GET", "POST", "PUT", "DELETE", "OPTIONS"));
    //Allowed headers
    config.setAllowedHeaders(List.of("Authorization", "Content-Type"));
    //Allow credentials (cookies, authorization headers)
    config.setAllowCredentials(true);

    UrlBasedCorsConfigurationSource source
         = new UrlBasedCorsConfigurationSource();
    //Apply CORS to all endpoints
    source.registerCorsConfiguration("/**", config);
    return source;
  }
}
```

LISTING 7-4: SecurityConfig.java

Here, we have allowed all kinds of methods and headers, but we can be more restrictive and specify only a subset of them to be allowed to access the API.

Also note that we have disabled *CSRF (Cross-Site Request Forgery)* protection. This is typically done in stateless REST APIs because such APIs don't use sessions or rely on cookies, which are the main targets of CSRF attacks.

Moreover, we have configured the authorization for incoming HTTP requests, by allowing all requests to be accessed without authentication (permitAll()) for the time being.

On the frontend side, we proceed with modifying ItemService class, so that it gets products from the API and not from a dummy list:

```
import { Injectable, } from '@angular/core';
import { Observable, catchError, of } from 'rxjs';
import { Item } from '../models/item';
import { ItemPayload } from '../models/itemPayload';
```

```typescript
import { Filter } from '../models/filter';
import { HttpClient, HttpHeaders, HttpParams } from '@angular/common/http';
import { environment } from '../../environments/environment';

@Injectable({
  providedIn: 'root'
})
export class ItemService {

  itemsUrl = `${environment.apiUrl}/items`;

  httpOptions = {
    headers: new HttpHeaders({ 'Content-Type': 'application/json' })
  };

  getItems(page: number, pageSize: number, filter: Filter)
    : Observable<ItemPayload> {
    let categoriesString: string = "";
    filter.categories
      .forEach(cc => categoriesString = categoriesString + cc + "#");
    if (categoriesString.length > 0)
      categoriesString = categoriesString
        .substring(0, categoriesString.length - 1);

    let params = new HttpParams()
      .set("name", filter.name)
      .set("pageNumber", page.toString())
      .set("pageSize", pageSize.toString())
      .set("category", categoriesString);

    return this.http.get<ItemPayload>(this.itemsUrl, { params: params })
      .pipe(
        catchError(this.handleError<ItemPayload>('getItems',
          { items: [], count: 0 }))
      );
  }

  getItem(id: number): Observable<Item> {
    const url = `${this.itemsUrl}/${id}`;
    return this.http.get<Item>(url)
      .pipe(
        catchError(this.handleError<Item>(`getItem/${id}`,
          { id: 0, name: "", price: 0, category: "", description: "" }))
      );
  }

  handleError<T>(operation = 'operation', result?: T) {
    return (error: any): Observable<T> => {
      console.error(error);
      return of(result as T);
    }
  }

  constructor(private http: HttpClient) { }
}
```

LISTING 7-5: item.service.ts

We should also add `HttpClientModule` in the imports section in *app.module.ts*.

Also, we should define the `apiUrl` parameter inside environments.ts:

```
export const environment = {
  production: false,
  apiUrl: 'http://localhost:8080'
};
```

LISTING 7-6: environment.development.ts

After Angular 15, we have to create the `environments` folder ourselves, with:

`ng g environments`

from the *src* folder.

Now, the Angular frontend loads the products list and information from the Spring Boot Web API.

You can find the code for this chapter in Github:

https://github.com/htset/htset-eshop-angular-18-spring/tree/part7

8. Authentication

In this chapter we will continue with the implementation of user authentication functionality in our Angular web app.

Frontend

On the Angular side, we first create the login component:

```html
<div class="col-md-6 offset-md-3 mt-5">
  <div class="card">
    <h4 class="card-header">Log in</h4>
    <div class="card-body">
      <form [formGroup]="loginForm" (ngSubmit)="onSubmit()">
        <div class="form-group">
          <label for="username">Username</label>
          <input type="text" formControlName="username"
              class="form-control" [ngClass]="{ 'is-invalid': submitted &&
                  loginForm.controls['username'].errors }" />
          <div *ngIf="submitted && loginForm.controls['username'].errors">
            <div *ngIf="loginForm.controls['username'].errors?.['required']">
              Required
            </div>
          </div>
        </div>
        <div class="form-group">
          <label for="password">Password</label>
          <input type="password" formControlName="password"
              class="form-control" [ngClass]="{ 'is-invalid': submitted &&
                  loginForm.controls['password'].errors }" />
          <div *ngIf="submitted && loginForm.controls['password'].errors">
            <div *ngIf="loginForm.controls['password'].errors?.['required']">
              Required
            </div>
          </div>
        </div>
        <button [disabled]="loading" class="btn btn-primary" id="login">
          <span *ngIf="loading"
              class="spinner-border spinner-border-sm mr-1"></span>
          Log in
        </button>
        <div *ngIf="error" class="alert alert-danger mt-3 mb-3">{{error}}</div>
      </form>
    </div>
  </div>
</div>
```

LISTING 8-1: login.component.html

The login form is implemented using Reactive Forms, so be sure to add the corresponding import (ReactiveFormsModule) in *app.module.ts*:

```
@NgModule({
...
  imports: [
...
    ReactiveFormsModule
  ],
  providers: [],
  bootstrap: [AppComponent]
})
export class AppModule { }
```

LISTING 8-2: app.module.ts

LoginComponent class defines a `FormGroup` that contains the two input fields (username and password). Those fields will be marked as "required" during validation on form submit.

```
import { Component, OnInit } from '@angular/core';
import { FormBuilder, FormGroup, Validators } from '@angular/forms';
import { ActivatedRoute, Router } from '@angular/router';
import            {            AuthenticationService            }            from
'../../../services/authentication.service';

@Component({
  selector: 'app-login',
  templateUrl: './login.component.html',
  styleUrls: ['./login.component.css']
})
export class LoginComponent implements OnInit {

  loginForm: FormGroup = new FormGroup({});
  loading: boolean = false;
  submitted: boolean = false;
  error: string = '';

  constructor(
    private formBuilder: FormBuilder,
    public authenticationService: AuthenticationService,
    public route: ActivatedRoute,
    public router: Router
  ) { }

  ngOnInit() {
    this.loginForm = this.formBuilder.group({
      username: ['', Validators.required],
      password: ['', Validators.required]
    });
  }

  onSubmit() {
    this.submitted = true;

    if (this.loginForm.invalid)
      return;
```

```
      this.loading = true;
      this.authenticationService.login(
        this.loginForm.controls['username'].value,
        this.loginForm.controls['password'].value
      )
        .subscribe({
          next: () => {
            const returnUrl
              = this.route.snapshot.queryParams['returnUrl'] || '/';
            this.router.navigate([returnUrl]);
          },
          error: error => {
            this.error = error.error;
            this.loading = false;
          }
        });
    }
}
```

LISTING 8-3: login.component.ts

We can see that, in onSubmit(), we call the login() method of a new service (AuthenticationService):

```
import { HttpClient } from '@angular/common/http';
import { Injectable } from '@angular/core';
import { map } from 'rxjs/operators';
import { environment } from '../../environments/environment';
import { User } from '../models/user';
import { StoreService } from './store.service';

@Injectable({
  providedIn: 'root'
})
export class AuthenticationService {

  constructor(
    public storeService: StoreService,
    private http: HttpClient
  ) { }

  login(username: string, password: string) {
    return this.http.post<User>(`${environment.apiUrl}/auth/login`,
      { username, password })
      .pipe(
        map(user => {
          sessionStorage.setItem('user', JSON.stringify(user));
          this.storeService.user = user;
          return user;
        })
      );
  }
```

```
  logout() {
    this.storeService.cart.emptyCart();
    sessionStorage.removeItem('user');
    this.storeService.user = null;
  }
}
```

LISTING 8-4: authentication.service.ts

AuthenticationService calls the backend RESTful method (/auth/login) which, on success, returns a User object. This object contains all information about the user that is stored in our database. Moreover, it contains a JWT Authentication Token that will be used in all subsequent requests.

The User object is stringified and stored in the sessionStorage, so that it will be available upon page reload. It is also stored in the StoreService object, so that will be available to all objects in the application:

```
....
  private readonly _user
    = new BehaviorSubject<User|null>(
        (sessionStorage.getItem('user')===null) ?
          null : JSON.parse(sessionStorage.getItem('user') ?? "")
      );
  readonly user$ = this._user.asObservable();

  get user(): User|null {
    return this._user.getValue();
  }

  set user(val: User|null) {
    this._user.next(val);
  }
....
```

LISTING 8-5: store.service.ts

Note that the BehaviorSubject object can also receive a null value (when there is no user logged in the application).

The User object has the following form:

```
export class User {
  id?: number;
  username?: string;
  password?: string;
  firstName?: string;
  lastName?: string;
  token?: string;
```

```
  role?: string;
  email?: string;
  status?: string;
}
```

LISTING 8-6: user.ts

Next, we need to add the routing entry for the Log in component:

```
...
const routes: Routes = [
  {path: '', component: ItemsComponent },
  {path: 'items', component: ItemsComponent },
  {path: 'items/:id', component: ItemDetailsComponent } ,
  {path: 'cart', component: CartComponent},
  {path: 'login', component: LoginComponent},
];
...
```

LISTING 8-7: app-routing.module.ts

Finally, we may add links to log in/log out, as well as current user information on all pages, through AppComponent:

```
@if (!user?.id){
<div align="right">
  <a routerLink='login'>Log in</a>
</div>
}

@if (storeService.cart.cartItems.length > 0){
<div align="right">
  <a routerLink='cart'>Cart</a>
</div>
}

@if (user?.id){
<div align="right">
  User: {{user?.username}} |
  <a href="#" (click)="logout($event)">Logout</a>
</div>
}

<router-outlet></router-outlet>
```

LISTING 8-8: app.component.html

Note that we are using the new @if directive in the place of *ngIf.

```
import { Component } from '@angular/core';
```

```typescript
import { StoreService } from './services/store.service';
import { AuthenticationService } from './services/authentication.service';
import { Router } from '@angular/router';
import { User } from './models/user';

@Component({
  selector: 'app-root',
  templateUrl: './app.component.html',
  styleUrls: ['./app.component.css']
})
export class AppComponent {

  user: User | null = null;

  constructor(
    private router: Router,
    public authenticationService: AuthenticationService,
    public storeService: StoreService
  ) {
    this.storeService.user$.subscribe(x => this.user = x);
  }

  logout(e: Event) {
    e.preventDefault();
    this.authenticationService.logout();
    this.router.navigate(['/login']);
  }
}
```

LISTING 8-9: app.component.ts

Backend

On the Web API side, we will have to implement the authentication method that our frontend calls during log in. For this purpose, we will first add JSON Web Token dependencies in pur *pom.xml* file:

```xml
<dependency>
  <groupId>io.jsonwebtoken</groupId>
  <artifactId>jjwt-api</artifactId>
  <version>0.11.5</version>
</dependency>
<dependency>
  <groupId>io.jsonwebtoken</groupId>
  <artifactId>jjwt-impl</artifactId>
  <version>0.11.5</version>
  <scope>runtime</scope>
</dependency>
<dependency>
  <groupId>io.jsonwebtoken</groupId>
  <artifactId>jjwt-jackson</artifactId>
```

```xml
    <version>0.11.5</version>
</dependency>
```

LISTING 8-10: pom.xml

Make sure you refresh the Maven project. Afterwards, we will create our model, the User class:

```java
package com.example.Eshop.models;

import jakarta.persistence.*;
import lombok.*;

@Data
@NoArgsConstructor
@AllArgsConstructor
@Entity
public class User {
  @Id
  @GeneratedValue(strategy = GenerationType.IDENTITY)
  private Long id;
  private String username;
  private String password;
  private String firstName;
  private String lastName;
  private String email;
  private String status;
  private String role;
  private String token;
}
```

LISTING 8-11: User.java

Next, we add the necessary repository to retrieve users from the database:

```java
package com.example.Eshop.repositories;

import com.example.Eshop.models.User;
import org.springframework.data.jpa.repository.JpaRepository;

public interface UserRepository extends JpaRepository<User, Long> {
  User findByUsername(String username);
}
```

LISTING 8-12: UserRepository.java

Next, we will implement a new controller that will handle the authentication process:

```java
package com.example.Eshop.controllers;
```

```java
import com.example.Eshop.config.JwtUtilities;
import com.example.Eshop.dtos.AuthRequestDTO;
import com.example.Eshop.dtos.CustomUserDetails;
import com.example.Eshop.dtos.UserDTO;
import com.example.Eshop.models.User;
import com.example.Eshop.services.CustomUserDetailsService;
import com.example.Eshop.services.UserService;
import org.springframework.http.HttpStatus;
import org.springframework.http.ResponseEntity;
import org.springframework.security.authentication.AuthenticationManager;
import org.springframework.security.authentication.BadCredentialsException;
import org.springframework.security.authentication.UsernamePasswordAuthenticationToken;
import org.springframework.security.core.userdetails.UsernameNotFoundException;
import org.springframework.security.crypto.password.PasswordEncoder;
import org.springframework.web.bind.annotation.PostMapping;
import org.springframework.web.bind.annotation.RequestBody;
import org.springframework.web.bind.annotation.RequestMapping;
import org.springframework.web.bind.annotation.RestController;

@RestController
@RequestMapping("/auth")
public class AuthController {
  private AuthenticationManager authenticationManager;
  private CustomUserDetailsService userDetailsService;
  private UserService userService;
  private JwtUtilities jwtUtilities;
  private PasswordEncoder passwordEncoder;

  public AuthController(AuthenticationManager authenticationManager,
                        CustomUserDetailsService userDetailsService,
                        UserService userService, JwtUtilities jwtUtilities,
                        PasswordEncoder passwordEncoder){
    this.authenticationManager = authenticationManager;
    this.userDetailsService = userDetailsService;
    this.userService = userService;
    this.jwtUtilities = jwtUtilities;
    this.passwordEncoder = passwordEncoder;
  }

  @PostMapping("/login")
  public ResponseEntity<?> login(@RequestBody AuthRequestDTO authRequest)
      throws Exception {
    //Use username and password to authenticate user
    try {
      authenticationManager.authenticate(
          new UsernamePasswordAuthenticationToken(authRequest.getUsername(),
            authRequest.getPassword())
      );

      CustomUserDetails userDetails =
          (CustomUserDetails)userDetailsService
              .loadUserByUsername(authRequest.getUsername());

      //Generate JWT token
```

```java
        String token = jwtUtilities.generateToken(userDetails.getUsername(),
            userDetails.getId(), userDetails.getRole());

        //Save token to database
        User user = userService.getUserById(userDetails.getId());
        user.setToken(token);
        userService.updateUser(user);

        return ResponseEntity.ok(this.createDTO(user));
    } catch (BadCredentialsException e) {
        return ResponseEntity.status(HttpStatus.UNAUTHORIZED)
            .body("Invalid credentials");
    } catch (UsernameNotFoundException e) {
        return ResponseEntity.status(HttpStatus.UNAUTHORIZED)
            .body("Invalid credentials");
    } catch (Exception e) {
        return ResponseEntity.status(HttpStatus.INTERNAL_SERVER_ERROR)
            .body("Authentication failed: " + e.getMessage());
    }
  }

  //Create user DTO for the response
  private UserDTO createDTO(User user){
    UserDTO userResponse = new UserDTO();
    userResponse.setId(user.getId());
    userResponse.setUsername(user.getUsername());
    userResponse.setStatus(user.getStatus());
    userResponse.setRole(user.getRole());
    userResponse.setToken(user.getToken());
    return userResponse;
  }
}
```

LISTING 8-13: AuthController.java

The login() method first verifies that the user exists and that the supplied password matches the one stored in the database. Upon success, it creates a JWT Authentication Token and returns it to the caller (along with the user information stored in the database).

We use a claims-based authentication scheme, where the user ID is stored inside the token and is used in the backend to identify the user.

The controller makes use of the CustomUserDetailsService class. This class implements interface org.springframework.security.core.userdetails.UserDetailsService, which is a core interface in Spring Security used for loading user-specific data. UserDetailsService allows us to integrate our authentication logic seamlessly with Spring Security's framework, as Spring Security uses UserDetailsService to load user details when a user tries to authenticate:

```
package com.example.Eshop.services;
```

```java
import com.example.Eshop.dtos.CustomUserDetails;
import com.example.Eshop.models.User;
import com.example.Eshop.repositories.UserRepository;
import org.springframework.security.core.userdetails.UsernameNotFoundException;
import org.springframework.security.crypto.password.PasswordEncoder;
import org.springframework.stereotype.Service;
import org.springframework.security.core.userdetails.UserDetailsService;

@Service
public class CustomUserDetailsService implements UserDetailsService {
  private UserRepository userRepository;
  private final PasswordEncoder passwordEncoder;

  public CustomUserDetailsService(UserRepository userRepository,
                                  PasswordEncoder passwordEncoder) {
    this.userRepository = userRepository;
    this.passwordEncoder = passwordEncoder;
  }

  @Override
  public CustomUserDetails loadUserByUsername(String username)
      throws UsernameNotFoundException {
    //Get user from the database
    User user = userRepository.findByUsername(username);
    if (user == null) {
      throw new UsernameNotFoundException("User not found: " + username);
    }

    //Return the custom UserDetails implementation
    return new CustomUserDetails(user);
  }
}
```

LISTING 8-14: CustomUserDetailsService.java

For this service, we also define class `CustomUserDetails` that implements the `org.springframework.security.core.userdetails.UserDetails` interface:

```java
package com.example.Eshop.dtos;

import com.example.Eshop.models.User;
import lombok.Data;
import org.springframework.security.core.GrantedAuthority;
import org.springframework.security.core.authority.SimpleGrantedAuthority;
import org.springframework.security.core.userdetails.UserDetails;
import java.util.ArrayList;
import java.util.Collection;
import java.util.Collections;

@Data
public class CustomUserDetails implements UserDetails {
  private Long id;
  private String username;
```

```java
    private String password;
    private String role;
    private String status;
    private String token;
    private Collection<GrantedAuthority> authorities;

    public CustomUserDetails(User user) {
      this.id = user.getId();
      this.username = user.getUsername();
      this.password = user.getPassword();
      this.role = user.getRole();
      this.status = user.getStatus();
      this.token = user.getToken();
      this.authorities = new ArrayList<GrantedAuthority>();
      this.authorities.add(new SimpleGrantedAuthority(user.getRole()));
    }

    @Override
    public Collection<? extends GrantedAuthority> getAuthorities() {
      return authorities != null ? authorities : Collections.emptyList();
    }

    @Override
    public boolean isAccountNonExpired() {
      return true;
    }

    @Override
    public boolean isAccountNonLocked() {
      return true;
    }

    @Override
    public boolean isCredentialsNonExpired() {
      return true;
    }

    @Override
    public boolean isEnabled() {
      if(status.equals("active"))
        return true;
      else
        return false;
    }
}
```

LISTING 8-15: CustomUserDetails.java

UserDetails is an interface provided by Spring Security that represents a user in the system. It holds essential information about the user, such as the username, password, and authorities (roles or permissions), which are used by Spring Security during authentication and authorization processes. `UserDetails` serves as a standard way to represent user data across various authentication methods supported by Spring Security.

The authentication controller also makes use of a `UserService` class, that provides access to the users in the database:

```java
package com.example.Eshop.services;

import com.example.Eshop.models.User;
import com.example.Eshop.repositories.UserRepository;
import org.springframework.stereotype.Service;

@Service
public class UserService {
  private UserRepository userRepository;
  public UserService(UserRepository userRepository) {
    this.userRepository = userRepository;
  }

  public User getUserById(Long id) {
    return userRepository.findById(id)
        .orElseThrow(() -> new RuntimeException("User not found"));
  }

  public User updateUser(User user) {
    return userRepository.save(user);   //Save or update the user
  }
}
```

LISTING 8-16: UserService.java

Having a separate `UserService` in addition to `UserDetailsService` provides several benefits in a Spring Boot application, especially when dealing with user management. While `UserDetailsService` focuses on loading user data for authentication purposes, `UserService` can offer additional functionalities that are essential for a comprehensive user management system (e.g. updating the user info).

The `login()` method of the authentication controller returns an object of type `UserDTO`. We use this *Data Transfer Object* to transmit user information back to the frontend, so that we can avoid sending back the full `User` object (along with the user' password, or other sensitive information).

```java
package com.example.Eshop.dtos;

import lombok.AllArgsConstructor;
import lombok.Data;
import lombok.NoArgsConstructor;

@Data
@NoArgsConstructor
@AllArgsConstructor
```

```java
public class UserDTO {

    private Long id;
    private String username;
    private String status;
    private String role;
    private String token;
}
```

LISTING 8-17: UserDTO.java

We have defined another DTO, that is used by the frontend to send the username and password:

```java
package com.example.Eshop.dtos;

import lombok.Data;

@Data
public class AuthRequestDTO {
    private String username;
    private String password;
}
```

LISTING 8-18: AuthRequestDTO.java

Another class that the authentication controller uses is the JwtUtilities class, that handles token creation:

```java
package com.example.Eshop.config;

import io.jsonwebtoken.Jwts;
import io.jsonwebtoken.SignatureAlgorithm;
import io.jsonwebtoken.security.Keys;
import org.springframework.stereotype.Component;
import javax.crypto.SecretKey;
import java.util.Date;
import java.util.HashMap;
import java.util.Map;

@Component
public class JwtUtilities {
    private final SecretKey secretKey
        = Keys.secretKeyFor(SignatureAlgorithm.HS512);

    //Generate token with user claims (username, userId, role)
    public String generateToken(String username, Long userId, String role) {
        Map<String, Object> claims = new HashMap<>();
        claims.put("userId", userId);
        claims.put("roles", role);
        return createToken(claims, username);
```

```java
    }
    //Create the token with the given claims and subject (username)
    public String createToken(Map<String, Object> claims, String subject) {
      return Jwts.builder()
          .setClaims(claims)
          .setSubject(subject)
          .setIssuedAt(new Date(System.currentTimeMillis()))
          //Token valid for 12 hours
          .setExpiration(new Date(System.currentTimeMillis()
              + 1000 * 60 * 60 * 12))
          .signWith(secretKey, SignatureAlgorithm.HS512)
          .compact();
    }
}
```

LISTING 8-19: JwtUtilities.java

In the subsequent chapters, this class will be updated with additional functionality for validating tokens, and more.

Finally, we have to update the security configuration of our project, so that authentication will work. More specifically, we add two new beans to *SecurityConfig.java*:

```java
package com.example.Eshop.config;

import org.springframework.security.authentication.AuthenticationManager;
import org.springframework.security.config.annotation.authentication.configuration.AuthenticationConfiguration;
import org.springframework.security.config.annotation.web.configuration.EnableWebSecurity;
import org.springframework.context.annotation.Bean;
import org.springframework.context.annotation.Configuration;
import org.springframework.security.config.annotation.web.builders.HttpSecurity;
import org.springframework.security.crypto.bcrypt.BCryptPasswordEncoder;
import org.springframework.security.crypto.password.PasswordEncoder;
import org.springframework.security.web.SecurityFilterChain;
import org.springframework.web.cors.CorsConfiguration;
import org.springframework.web.cors.UrlBasedCorsConfigurationSource;
import java.util.List;

@Configuration
@EnableWebSecurity
public class SecurityConfig {

  @Bean
  public SecurityFilterChain securityFilterChain(HttpSecurity http)
      throws Exception {
    http
        //Disable CSRF since this is a stateless REST API
        .csrf(csrf -> csrf.disable())
        //Enable CORS
```

```java
        .cors(cors -> cors.configurationSource(corsConfigurationSource()))
        //Access all endpoints without authentication - for now
        .authorizeHttpRequests(auth -> auth
                .anyRequest().permitAll()
        );
    return http.build();
}

@Bean
public UrlBasedCorsConfigurationSource corsConfigurationSource() {
    CorsConfiguration config = new CorsConfiguration();
    //Allowed origins
    config.setAllowedOrigins(List.of("http://localhost:4200"));
    //Allowed HTTP methods
    config.setAllowedMethods(List.of("GET", "POST", "PUT", "DELETE", "OPTIONS"));
    //Allowed headers
    config.setAllowedHeaders(List.of("Authorization", "Content-Type"));
    //Allow credentials (cookies, authorization headers)
    config.setAllowCredentials(true);

    UrlBasedCorsConfigurationSource source
            = new UrlBasedCorsConfigurationSource();
    //Apply CORS to all endpoints
    source.registerCorsConfiguration("/**", config);
    return source;
}

@Bean
public AuthenticationManager
    authenticationManager(AuthenticationConfiguration authConfiguration)
        throws Exception {
    return authConfiguration.getAuthenticationManager();
}

@Bean
public PasswordEncoder passwordEncoder() {
    return new BCryptPasswordEncoder();
}
}
```

LISTING 8-20: SecurityConfig.java

The `AuthenticationManager` is a key component in Spring Security authentication mechanism, as it is responsible for processing authentication requests and determining whether a user is authenticated or not.

The purpose of the `PasswordEncoder` bean is to securely hash passwords before storing them in a database and to compare user-submitted passwords during authentication using the BCrypt hashing algorithm. It includes a built-in mechanism for salting, which helps protect against dictionary attacks and rainbow table attacks.

The above solution focuses solely on the authentication of a user, i.e. checking the user's credentials against those stored in a database and sending a JWT Token that will be eventually stored in the Session Storage.

We can test this code with a couple of users that we will insert into the database:

```
insert into user(first_name, last_name, username, password,
role, email, token, status)
values
('user', 'user', 'user',
'$2a$10$Bw3CUtDVZ0RLAQHwFNANA.jSDDU7X9Wdse6uM4qXusgs4/kK2qOWK',
  'CUSTOMER', 'user@test.com', 'xx', 'ACTIVE'),
('admin', 'admin', 'admin',
'$2a$10$Bw3CUtDVZ0RLAQHwFNANA.jSDDU7X9Wdse6uM4qXusgs4/kK2qOWK',
  'ADMIN', 'admin@test.com', 'xx', 'ACTIVE')
```

LISTING 8-21: SQL code

The password for both users is '1234'.

You may find the code for this chapter here:

https://github.com/htset/htset-eshop-angular-18-spring/tree/part8

9. Authorization

In this chapter, we complement the authentication functionality by introducing authorization to our project.

Frontend

First of all, we add a new folder (named helpers) that will contain helper classes for authorization and other stuff.

Inside the helpers folder we create an interceptor class:

```
import { Injectable } from "@angular/core";
import { HttpEvent, HttpHandler, HttpInterceptor, HttpRequest }
  from "@angular/common/http";
import { Observable } from "rxjs";
import { environment } from "../../environments/environment";
import { StoreService } from "../services/store.service";

@Injectable()
export class JwtInterceptor implements HttpInterceptor {
  constructor(private storeService: StoreService) { }

  intercept(request: HttpRequest<any>, next: HttpHandler):
    Observable<HttpEvent<any>> {
    const currentUser = this.storeService.user;
    const isLoggedIn = currentUser && currentUser.token;
    const isApiUrl = request.url.startsWith(environment.apiUrl);
    if (isLoggedIn && isApiUrl) {
      request = request.clone({
        setHeaders: {
          Authorization: `Bearer ${currentUser?.token}`
        }
      });
    }
    return next.handle(request);
  }
}
```

LISTING 9-1: jwt.interceptor.ts

This class contains a single function that gets called for every outgoing http request (to the API only). If the user has already logged in, this function will add a JSON Web Token in the request header. This token was sent by the backend during the authentication phase and was stored in session storage, as we already saw in the previous chapter.

The token is inspected by the backend API in order to decide whether the request for data is authorized or not.

Make sure you declare the interceptor class in the providers section of *app.module.ts*:

```
...
  providers: [
    provideAnimationsAsync(),
    {
      provide: HTTP_INTERCEPTORS,
      useClass: JwtInterceptor, multi: true
    }
  ],
...
```

LISTING 9-2: app.module.ts

Next, inside the admin folder (src/app/components/admin) we create two new components:

- admin-home
- admin-users

The admin-home component contains the menu for the admin pages and provides the router outlet for the display of the other admin components that we will create:

```
<h2>Admin pages</h2>
<nav class="navbar navbar-light"
    style="background-color: #e3f2fd;">
  <a class="nav-item nav-link"
    routerLink="/admin/users">Users</a>
</nav>
<router-outlet></router-outlet>
```

LISTING 9-3: admin-home.component.html

The admin-users component displays info about all users:

```
<h3>Users</h3>
<div class="card-body">
  @if(users){
  <table class="table table-striped">
    <tr>
      <th>ID</th>
      <th>Username</th>
      <th>First Name</th>
      <th>Last Name</th>
      <th>Role</th>
      <th>Email</th>
    </tr>
    @for(user of users; track user.id){
      <tr>
        <td>{{user.id}}</td>
        <td>{{user.username}}</td>
        <td>{{user.firstName}}</td>
        <td>{{user.lastName}}</td>
        <td>{{user.role}}</td>
        <td>{{user.email}}</td>
```

```
      </tr>
    }
  </table>
  }
</div>
```

LISTING 9-4: admin-users.component.html


```
import { Component, OnInit } from '@angular/core';
import { User } from '../../../models/user';
import { UserService } from '../../../services/user.service';

@Component({
  selector: 'app-admin-users',
  templateUrl: './admin-users.component.html',
  styleUrl: './admin-users.component.css'
})
export class AdminUsersComponent implements OnInit {

  users!: User[];

  constructor(private userService: UserService) { }

  ngOnInit() {
    this.userService.getAllUsers().subscribe(
      ((users: User[]) => {
        this.users = users;
      }),
      ((err: any) => {
        console.log(err);
      }));
  }
}
```

LISTING 9-5: admin-users.component.ts

The admin-users component makes use of a new service, UserService that communicates with the backend API:

```
import { HttpClient, HttpHeaders } from '@angular/common/http';
import { Injectable } from '@angular/core';
import { User } from '../models/user';
import { environment } from '../../environments/environment';

@Injectable({
  providedIn: 'root'
})
export class UserService {

  httpOptions = {
    headers: new HttpHeaders({ 'Content-Type': 'application/json' })
  };
```

```
  constructor(private http: HttpClient) { }

  getAllUsers() {
    return this.http.get<User[]>(`${environment.apiUrl}/users`);
  }
}
```

LISTING 9-6: user.service.ts

Access to the admin components should be allowed only to users of type ADMIN. We achieve this with the use of a *guard class* (*auth.guard.ts*), that we create inside the helpers folder:

```
import { Injectable } from "@angular/core";
import { ActivatedRouteSnapshot, CanActivate, Router, RouterStateSnapshot }
  from "@angular/router";
import { StoreService } from "../services/store.service";

@Injectable({ providedIn: 'root' })
export class AuthGuard implements CanActivate {
  constructor(
    private router: Router,
    private storeService: StoreService
  ) { }

  canActivate(route: ActivatedRouteSnapshot, state: RouterStateSnapshot) {
    const currentUser = this.storeService.user;
    if (currentUser && currentUser.role == 'ADMIN') {
      return true;
    }
    else if (currentUser && currentUser.role == 'CUSTOMER') {
      this.router.navigate(['/items']);
      return true;
    }

    this.router.navigate(['/login'], { queryParams: { returnUrl: state.url } });
    return false;
  }
}
```

LISTING 9-7: auth.guard.ts

The canActivate() function in the guard class is called whenever access to a protected route is requested. We designate routes as protected in *app-routing.module.ts*:

```
import { NgModule } from '@angular/core';
import { RouterModule, Routes } from '@angular/router';
import { ItemsComponent } from './components/public/items/items.component';
import { ItemDetailsComponent }
  from './components/public/item-details/item-details.component';
import { CartComponent } from './components/public/cart/cart.component';
```

```typescript
import { LoginComponent } from './components/public/login/login.component';
import { AdminHomeComponent }
  from './components/admin/admin-home/admin-home.component';
import { AuthGuard } from './helpers/auth.guard';
import { AdminUsersComponent }
  from './components/admin/admin-users/admin-users.component';

const routes: Routes = [
  { path: '', component: ItemsComponent },
  { path: 'items', component: ItemsComponent },
  { path: 'items/:id', component: ItemDetailsComponent },
  { path: 'cart', component: CartComponent },
  { path: 'login', component: LoginComponent },
  {
    path: 'admin', component: AdminHomeComponent,
    canActivate: [AuthGuard],
    children: [
      { path: 'users', component: AdminUsersComponent }
    ]
  },
];

@NgModule({
  imports: [RouterModule.forRoot(routes)],
  exports: [RouterModule]
})
export class AppRoutingModule { }
```

LISTING 9-8: app-routing.module.ts

We see that access to the /admin route will result in the invocation of the canActivate() function in AuthGuard class. This function checks whether the user is logged in and of type ADMIN and only then allows access to the /admin route.

Note also, the way that we define children routes (e.g. /admin/users). The guard restrictions apply also to all those routes.

Backend

We will start with the JSON Web Token processing. As we saw earlier, each HTTP request to the backend will contain a JWT in the header. The task of the middleware is to extract the token and verify that it is valid.

In addition to that, the backend will extract from the token the role of the user (ADMIN or CUSTOMER). Based on the role, we will be able to authorize or not the access to a specific REST resource.

Next, we configure a request filter that will be used to extract the Token from the incoming request and validate it:

```
package com.example.Eshop.config;
```

```java
import org.springframework.security.authentication.UsernamePasswordAuthenticationToken;
import org.springframework.security.core.context.SecurityContextHolder;
import org.springframework.security.core.userdetails.UserDetails;
import org.springframework.security.core.userdetails.UserDetailsService;
import org.springframework.security.web.authentication.WebAuthenticationDetailsSource;
import org.springframework.stereotype.Component;
import org.springframework.web.filter.OncePerRequestFilter;
import jakarta.servlet.FilterChain;
import jakarta.servlet.ServletException;
import jakarta.servlet.http.HttpServletRequest;
import jakarta.servlet.http.HttpServletResponse;
import java.io.IOException;

@Component
public class JwtRequestFilter extends OncePerRequestFilter {
  private final JwtUtilities jwtUtil;
  private final UserDetailsService myUserDetailsService;

  public JwtRequestFilter(JwtUtilities jwtUtil,
                          UserDetailsService myUserDetailsService) {
    this.jwtUtil = jwtUtil;
    this.myUserDetailsService = myUserDetailsService;
  }

  @Override
  protected void doFilterInternal(HttpServletRequest request,
                                  HttpServletResponse response,
                                  FilterChain chain)
      throws ServletException, IOException {

    //Skip filtering for login endpoint
    String path = request.getServletPath();
    if (path.equals("/auth/login")) {
      chain.doFilter(request, response);
      return;
    }

    final String authorizationHeader = request.getHeader("Authorization");
    String username = null;
    String jwt = null;

    // Extract JWT from the Authorization header (if present)
    if (authorizationHeader != null
        && authorizationHeader.startsWith("Bearer ")) {
      jwt = authorizationHeader.substring(7); //Remove "Bearer " prefix
      username = jwtUtil.extractUsername(jwt);
    }

    //Validate the token and set authentication
    if (username != null
        && SecurityContextHolder.getContext().getAuthentication() == null) {
      UserDetails userDetails
```

```java
          = this.myUserDetailsService.loadUserByUsername(username);

      if (jwtUtil.validateToken(jwt, userDetails.getUsername())) {
        UsernamePasswordAuthenticationToken authToken
            = new UsernamePasswordAuthenticationToken(
                userDetails, null, userDetails.getAuthorities());
        authToken.setDetails(new WebAuthenticationDetailsSource()
                                .buildDetails(request));
        SecurityContextHolder.getContext().setAuthentication(authToken);
      }
    }

    chain.doFilter(request, response);
  }
}
```

LISTING 9-9: JwtRequestFilter.java

The request filter uses specific methods to extract and validate the token. We should add them in JwtUtilities.java:

```java
package com.example.Eshop.config;

import io.jsonwebtoken.Claims;
import io.jsonwebtoken.Jwts;
import io.jsonwebtoken.SignatureAlgorithm;
import io.jsonwebtoken.security.Keys;
import org.springframework.stereotype.Component;
import javax.crypto.SecretKey;
import java.util.Date;
import java.util.HashMap;
import java.util.Map;
import java.util.function.Function;

@Component
public class JwtUtilities {
  private final SecretKey secretKey
      = Keys.secretKeyFor(SignatureAlgorithm.HS512);

  //Extract all claims from the token
  public Claims extractAllClaims(String token) {
    return Jwts.parserBuilder()
        .setSigningKey(secretKey)
        .build()
        .parseClaimsJws(token)
        .getBody();
  }

  //Extract a single claim from the token
  public <T> T extractClaim(String token,
                           Function<Claims, T> claimsResolver) {
    final Claims claims = extractAllClaims(token);
    return claimsResolver.apply(claims);
```

```java
    }

    public String extractUsername(String token) {
        return extractClaim(token, Claims::getSubject);
    }

    private Boolean isTokenExpired(String token) {
        return extractAllClaims(token)
            .getExpiration()
            .before(new Date());
    }

    //Generate token with user claims (username, userId, role)
    public String generateToken(String username,
                                Long userId, String role) {
        Map<String, Object> claims = new HashMap<>();
        claims.put("userId", userId);
        claims.put("roles", role);
        return createToken(claims, username);
    }

    //Create the token with the given claims and subject (username)
    public String createToken(Map<String, Object> claims,
                              String subject) {
        return Jwts.builder()
            .setClaims(claims)
            .setSubject(subject)
            .setIssuedAt(new Date(System.currentTimeMillis()))
            //Token valid for 12 hours
                    .setExpiration(new Date(System.currentTimeMillis()
                + 1000 * 60 * 60 * 12))
            .signWith(secretKey, SignatureAlgorithm.HS512)
            .compact();
    }

    //Validate the token by checking username and expiry
    public Boolean validateToken(String token, String username) {
        final String extractedUsername = extractUsername(token);
        return (extractedUsername.equals(username) && !isTokenExpired(token));
    }
}
```

LISTING 9-10: JwtUtilities.java

The request filter should be added in *SecurityConfig.java*:

```
package com.example.Eshop.config;

import org.springframework.security.authentication.AuthenticationManager;
import org.springframework.security.config.annotation.authentication.configuration.AuthenticationConfiguration;
import
```

```java
org.springframework.security.config.annotation.web.configuration.EnableWebSecurity;
import org.springframework.context.annotation.Bean;
import org.springframework.context.annotation.Configuration;
import org.springframework.security.config.annotation.web.builders.HttpSecurity;
import org.springframework.security.web.SecurityFilterChain;
import org.springframework.security.web.authentication.UsernamePasswordAuthenticationFilter;
import org.springframework.web.cors.CorsConfiguration;
import org.springframework.web.cors.UrlBasedCorsConfigurationSource;
import java.util.List;

@Configuration
@EnableWebSecurity
public class SecurityConfig {

  private final JwtRequestFilter jwtRequestFilter;
  private final JwtAuthenticationEntryPoint jwtAuthenticationEntryPoint;

  public SecurityConfig(JwtRequestFilter jwtRequestFilter,
                        JwtAuthenticationEntryPoint jwtAuthenticationEntryPoint) {
    this.jwtRequestFilter = jwtRequestFilter;
    this.jwtAuthenticationEntryPoint = jwtAuthenticationEntryPoint;
  }

  @Bean
  public SecurityFilterChain securityFilterChain(HttpSecurity http)
      throws Exception {
    http
        //Disable CSRF since this is a stateless REST API
        .csrf(csrf -> csrf.disable())
        //Enable CORS
        .cors(cors -> cors.configurationSource(corsConfigurationSource()))
        //Define public endpoints that can be accessed without authentication
        .authorizeHttpRequests(auth -> auth
                .requestMatchers("/users/**").hasRole("ADMIN")
                .requestMatchers(
                    "/auth/**",
                    "/items/**").permitAll()  // Allow access to auth endpoints
                .anyRequest().authenticated() // All other endpoints
                                              //   get authentication
        )
        //Add JWT token filter before UsernamePasswordAuthenticationFilter
        .addFilterBefore(jwtRequestFilter,
            UsernamePasswordAuthenticationFilter.class);

    return http.build();
  }

  @Bean
  public UrlBasedCorsConfigurationSource corsConfigurationSource() {
    CorsConfiguration config = new CorsConfiguration();
    //Allowed origins
    config.setAllowedOrigins(List.of("http://localhost:4200"));
    //Allowed HTTP methods
```

```
    config.setAllowedMethods(List.of("GET", "POST", "PUT", "DELETE", "OPTIONS"));
    //Allowed headers
    config.setAllowedHeaders(List.of("Authorization", "Content-Type"));
    //Allow credentials (cookies, authorization headers)
    config.setAllowCredentials(true);

    UrlBasedCorsConfigurationSource source
        = new UrlBasedCorsConfigurationSource();
    //Apply CORS to all endpoints
    source.registerCorsConfiguration("/**", config);
    return source;
  }

  @Bean
  public AuthenticationManager
    authenticationManager(AuthenticationConfiguration authConfiguration)
      throws Exception {
    return authConfiguration.getAuthenticationManager();
  }
}
```

LISTING 9-11: SecurityConfig.java

In the above snippet, note that we also updated the authorization policy on the RESTful resources. More specifically, the /users resource should only be accessed by administrators. Furthemore, the /auth and /items resources should be accessible without authentication, while all the other routes should be protected.

Also note that we had to move the PasswordEncoder bean to the EshopApplication class, as it introduced cyclic dependencies when it was included in *SecurityConfig.java*:

```
package com.example.Eshop;

import org.springframework.boot.SpringApplication;
import org.springframework.boot.autoconfigure.SpringBootApplication;
import org.springframework.context.annotation.Bean;
import org.springframework.security.crypto.bcrypt.BCryptPasswordEncoder;
import org.springframework.security.crypto.password.PasswordEncoder;

@SpringBootApplication
public class EshopApplication {
  @Bean
  public PasswordEncoder passwordEncoder() {
    return new BCryptPasswordEncoder();
  }

  public static void main(String[] args) {
    SpringApplication.run(EshopApplication.class, args);
  }

}
```

LISTING 9-12: EshopApplication.java

Next, we have to create a new class, `JwtAuthenticationEntryPoint` in the `config` package:

```
package com.example.Eshop.config;

import org.springframework.security.core.AuthenticationException;
import org.springframework.security.web.AuthenticationEntryPoint;
import org.springframework.stereotype.Component;
import jakarta.servlet.http.HttpServletRequest;
import jakarta.servlet.http.HttpServletResponse;
import java.io.IOException;

@Component
public class JwtAuthenticationEntryPoint implements AuthenticationEntryPoint {

  @Override
  public void commence(HttpServletRequest request,
                       HttpServletResponse response,
                       AuthenticationException authException)
      throws IOException {
    response.sendError(HttpServletResponse.SC_UNAUTHORIZED, "Unauthorized");
  }
}
```

LISTING 9-13: JwtAuthenticationEntryPoint.java

`JwtAuthenticationEntryPoint` is a component in a Spring Security configuration that handles unauthorized access attempts. It is used specifically when working with JSON Web Token authentication. When a user tries to access a secured resource without being authenticated, or with an invalid/expired JWT, the `JwtAuthenticationEntryPoint` triggers a response.

You may notice that `JwtAuthenticationEntryPoint` is injected into the constructor of `SecurityConfig` class.

To complete the authorization process, we need to make a little update in `CustomUserDetails` class:

```
package com.example.Eshop.dtos;

import com.example.Eshop.models.User;
import lombok.Data;
import org.springframework.security.core.GrantedAuthority;
import org.springframework.security.core.authority.SimpleGrantedAuthority;
import org.springframework.security.core.userdetails.UserDetails;
import java.util.ArrayList;
import java.util.Collection;
import java.util.Collections;

@Data
public class CustomUserDetails implements UserDetails {
```

```java
    private Long id;
    private String username;
    private String password;
    private String role;
    private String status;
    private String token;
    private Collection<GrantedAuthority> authorities;

    public CustomUserDetails(User user) {
        this.id = user.getId();
        this.username = user.getUsername();
        this.password = user.getPassword();
        this.role = user.getRole();
        this.status = user.getStatus();
        this.token = user.getToken();
        this.authorities = new ArrayList<GrantedAuthority>();
        this.authorities.add(new SimpleGrantedAuthority(user.getRole()));
    }

    @Override
    public Collection<? extends GrantedAuthority> getAuthorities() {
        String role = "ROLE_" + this.role;
        return Collections.singletonList(new SimpleGrantedAuthority(role));
    }

    @Override
    public boolean isAccountNonExpired() {
        return true;
    }

    @Override
    public boolean isAccountNonLocked() {
        return true;
    }

    @Override
    public boolean isCredentialsNonExpired() {
        return true;
    }

    @Override
    public boolean isEnabled() {
        if(status.equals("active"))
            return true;
        else
            return false;
    }
}
```

LISTING 9-14: CustomUserDetails.java

In our implementation, each user has only one role, either CUSTOMER or ADMIN. Method getAuthorities() returns a collection of GrantedAuthority objects (only one in our case) that represent the roles or privileges assigned to the user. These authorities are used by Spring Security to determine if the user is allowed to perform a particular action or access a specific resource (as we saw in SecurityConfig).

Method getAuthorities() adds the prefix ROLE_ to each role, as this is the expected role format in Spring Security.

Finally, we will create the UserController that will provide administrators with a list of users:

```
package com.example.Eshop.controllers;

import com.example.Eshop.models.User;
import com.example.Eshop.services.UserService;
import org.springframework.web.bind.annotation.*;
import java.util.List;

@RestController
@RequestMapping("/users")
public class UserController {

  private UserService userService;

  public UserController(UserService userService){
    this.userService = userService;
  }

  @GetMapping
  public List<User> getAllUsers() {
    return userService.getAllUsers();
  }

}
```

LISTING 9-15: UserController.java

We should also add the getAllUsers() method in UserService class:

```
package com.example.Eshop.services;

import com.example.Eshop.models.User;
import com.example.Eshop.repositories.UserRepository;
import org.springframework.stereotype.Service;
import java.util.List;

@Service
public class UserService {
  private UserRepository userRepository;
  public UserService(UserRepository userRepository) {
    this.userRepository = userRepository;
  }
```

```java
public User getUserById(Long id) {
  return userRepository.findById(id)
      .orElseThrow(() -> new RuntimeException("User not found"));
}

public List<User> getAllUsers(){
  return userRepository.findAll();
}

public User updateUser(User user) {
  return userRepository.save(user);   //Save or update the user
  }
}
```

LISTING 9-16: UserService.java

For testing, let's remove temporarily the `canActivate` parameter from file *app-routing.module.ts* in the Angular frontend and try to access directly the `admin/users` page. If we are not logged in, or we are logged in as customers, then we will get a *403 Forbidden*, which means that we do not have access to this resource.

You may find the code for this chapter here:

https://github.com/htset/htset-eshop-angular-18-spring/tree/part9

10. Authentication —Access token refresh/revoke

On this chapter, we will continue with the authentication stuff, and we will introduce the functionality to refresh a token upon its expiration. We will also enable the revocation of a token at user logout.

If you study the code about authentication, you will see that the access token has an expiration time of 12 hours, which is a very long time to keep the same token. Tokens should be short-lived and should be refreshed upon expiration, to ensure that our application remains secure.

To achieve this, we will use the following process: First, we will reduce the access token expiration time to 2 minutes. After the access token has expired, any attempt to access a protected route in the frontend (i.e. the admin part of the application) will result in a request to the API for a token refresh. After the access token has been refreshed successfully, it will replace the existing one, and the process will continue until the new token expires as well.

The token refresh operation requires the use of a new kind of token, the refresh token. This is a long random string that will stay the same for a much longer time (e.g. one week). When the frontend needs to refresh the access token, it will send the refresh token to the API as proof of its identity.

Backend

To start, we modify the `User` model, by adding the refresh token and its expiration time:

```java
package com.example.Eshop.models;

import jakarta.persistence.*;
import lombok.*;

import java.util.Date;

@Data
@NoArgsConstructor
@AllArgsConstructor
@Entity
public class User {
    @Id
    @GeneratedValue(strategy = GenerationType.IDENTITY)
    private Long id;
    private String username;
    private String password;
    private String firstName;
    private String lastName;
    private String email;
    private String status;
    private String role;
```

```
    private String token;
    private String refreshToken;
    private Date refreshTokenExpiry;
}
```

LISTING 10-1: User.java

We will update also the corresponding DTO:

```
package com.example.Eshop.dtos;

import lombok.AllArgsConstructor;
import lombok.Data;
import lombok.NoArgsConstructor;

import java.util.Date;

@Data
@NoArgsConstructor
@AllArgsConstructor
public class UserDTO {

    private Long id;
    private String username;
    private String status;
    private String role;
    private String token;
    private String refreshToken;
    private Date refreshTokenExpiry;
}
```

LISTING 10-2: UserDTO.java

Then, we add the two operations the authentication controller (`AuthController`):

```
package com.example.Eshop.controllers;

import com.example.Eshop.config.JwtUtilities;
import com.example.Eshop.dtos.AuthRequestDTO;
import com.example.Eshop.dtos.CustomUserDetails;
import com.example.Eshop.dtos.TokenRefreshDTO;
import com.example.Eshop.dtos.UserDTO;
import com.example.Eshop.models.User;
import com.example.Eshop.services.CustomUserDetailsService;
import com.example.Eshop.services.UserService;
import org.springframework.http.HttpStatus;
import org.springframework.http.ResponseEntity;
import org.springframework.security.authentication.AuthenticationManager;
import org.springframework.security.authentication.BadCredentialsException;
import org.springframework.security.authentication.UsernamePasswordAuthenticationToken;
import org.springframework.security.core.userdetails.UsernameNotFoundException;
```

```java
import org.springframework.security.crypto.password.PasswordEncoder;
import org.springframework.web.bind.annotation.PostMapping;
import org.springframework.web.bind.annotation.RequestBody;
import org.springframework.web.bind.annotation.RequestMapping;
import org.springframework.web.bind.annotation.RestController;

import java.util.Date;

@RestController
@RequestMapping("/auth")
public class AuthController {
  private AuthenticationManager authenticationManager;
  private CustomUserDetailsService userDetailsService;
  private UserService userService;
  private JwtUtilities jwtUtilities;
  private PasswordEncoder passwordEncoder;

  public AuthController(AuthenticationManager authenticationManager,
                        CustomUserDetailsService userDetailsService,
                        UserService userService, JwtUtilities jwtUtilities,
                        PasswordEncoder passwordEncoder){
    this.authenticationManager = authenticationManager;
    this.userDetailsService = userDetailsService;
    this.userService = userService;
    this.jwtUtilities = jwtUtilities;
    this.passwordEncoder = passwordEncoder;
  }

  @PostMapping("/login")
  public ResponseEntity<?> login(@RequestBody AuthRequestDTO authRequest)
      throws Exception {
    //Use username and password to authenticate user
    try {
      authenticationManager.authenticate(
          new UsernamePasswordAuthenticationToken(authRequest.getUsername(),
            authRequest.getPassword())
      );

      CustomUserDetails userDetails =
          (CustomUserDetails)userDetailsService
              .loadUserByUsername(authRequest.getUsername());

      //Generate JWT tokens
      String token = jwtUtilities.generateToken(userDetails.getUsername(),
          userDetails.getId(), userDetails.getRole());
      String refreshToken = jwtUtilities
          .generateRefreshToken(userDetails.getUsername());

      //Save token to database
      User user = userService.getUserById(userDetails.getId());
      user.setToken(token);
      user.setRefreshToken(refreshToken);
      user.setRefreshTokenExpiry(new Date(System.currentTimeMillis()
          + 1000L * 60 * 60 * 24 * 30)); // 30-day expiry
      userService.updateUser(user);
```

```java
      return ResponseEntity.ok(this.createDTO(user));
    } catch (BadCredentialsException e) {
      return ResponseEntity.status(HttpStatus.UNAUTHORIZED)
          .body("Invalid credentials");
    } catch (UsernameNotFoundException e) {
      return ResponseEntity.status(HttpStatus.UNAUTHORIZED)
          .body("Invalid credentials");
    } catch (Exception e) {
      return ResponseEntity.status(HttpStatus.INTERNAL_SERVER_ERROR)
          .body("Authentication failed: " + e.getMessage());
    }
  }

  @PostMapping("/refresh")
  public ResponseEntity<?> refreshToken(@RequestBody TokenRefreshDTO request) {
    try{
      String refreshToken = request.getRefreshToken();
      if (jwtUtilities.validateRefreshToken(refreshToken)) {
        String username = jwtUtilities.extractUsername(refreshToken);
        CustomUserDetails userDetails
            = userDetailsService.loadUserByUsername(username);

        //Generate new token
        String newToken = jwtUtilities.generateToken(userDetails.getUsername(),
            ((CustomUserDetails) userDetails).getId(), userDetails.getRole());

        //Save updated tokens to database
        User user = userService.getUserById(userDetails.getId());
        user.setToken(newToken);
        userService.updateUser(user);

        return ResponseEntity.ok(this.createDTO(user));
      } else {
        return ResponseEntity.status(HttpStatus.UNAUTHORIZED)
            .body("Invalid refresh token");
      }
    } catch (UsernameNotFoundException e) {
      return ResponseEntity.status(HttpStatus.NOT_FOUND)
          .body("User not found");
    } catch (Exception e) {
      return ResponseEntity.status(HttpStatus.INTERNAL_SERVER_ERROR)
          .body("Refresh token failed:" + e.getMessage());
    }
  }

  @PostMapping("/revoke")
  public ResponseEntity<?> revokeToken(@RequestBody TokenRefreshDTO request) {
    try {
      String refreshToken = request.getRefreshToken();
      if (jwtUtilities.validateRefreshToken(refreshToken)) {
        String username = jwtUtilities.extractUsername(refreshToken);
        CustomUserDetails userDetails
            = userDetailsService.loadUserByUsername(username);
```

```java
      //Revoke the tokens by setting them to null
      User user = userService.getUserById(userDetails.getId());
      user.setToken(null);
      user.setRefreshToken(null);
      user.setRefreshTokenExpiry(null);

      //Update the user in the database
      userService.updateUser(user);

      return ResponseEntity.ok(this.createDTO(user));
    } else {
      return ResponseEntity.status(HttpStatus.INTERNAL_SERVER_ERROR)
        .body("Error revoking token");
    }
  } catch (UsernameNotFoundException e) {
    return ResponseEntity.status(HttpStatus.NOT_FOUND)
      .body("User not found");
  } catch (Exception e) {
    return ResponseEntity.status(HttpStatus.INTERNAL_SERVER_ERROR)
      .body("Revoke token failed: " + e.getMessage());
  }
}

//Create user DTO for the response
private UserDTO createDTO(User user){
  UserDTO userResponse = new UserDTO();
  userResponse.setId(user.getId());
  userResponse.setUsername(user.getUsername());
  userResponse.setStatus(user.getStatus());
  userResponse.setRole(user.getRole());
  userResponse.setToken(user.getToken());
  userResponse.setRefreshToken(user.getRefreshToken());
  userResponse.setRefreshTokenExpiry(user.getRefreshTokenExpiry());
  return userResponse;
  }
}
```

LISTING 10-3: AuthController.java

We also add functionality to generate and validate a refresh token:

```java
package com.example.Eshop.config;

import io.jsonwebtoken.Claims;
import io.jsonwebtoken.ExpiredJwtException;
import io.jsonwebtoken.Jwts;
import io.jsonwebtoken.SignatureAlgorithm;
import io.jsonwebtoken.security.Keys;
import io.jsonwebtoken.security.SignatureException;
import org.springframework.stereotype.Component;
import javax.crypto.SecretKey;
import java.util.Date;
import java.util.HashMap;
```

```java
import java.util.Map;
import java.util.function.Function;

@Component
public class JwtUtilities {
  private final SecretKey secretKey
      = Keys.secretKeyFor(SignatureAlgorithm.HS512);

  //Extract all claims from the token
  public Claims extractAllClaims(String token) {
    return Jwts.parserBuilder()
        .setSigningKey(secretKey)
        .build()
        .parseClaimsJws(token)
        .getBody();
  }

  //Extract a single claim from the token
  public <T> T extractClaim(String token,
                            Function<Claims, T> claimsResolver) {
    final Claims claims = extractAllClaims(token);
    return claimsResolver.apply(claims);
  }

  public String extractUsername(String token) {
    return extractClaim(token, Claims::getSubject);
  }

  public Boolean isTokenExpired(String token) {
    return extractAllClaims(token)
        .getExpiration()
        .before(new Date());
  }

  //Generate token with user claims (username, userId, role)
  public String generateToken(String username,
                              Long userId, String role) {
    Map<String, Object> claims = new HashMap<>();
    claims.put("userId", userId);
    claims.put("roles", role);
    return createToken(claims, username);
  }

  //Create the token with the given claims and subject (username)
  public String createToken(Map<String, Object> claims,
                            String subject) {
    return Jwts.builder()
        .setClaims(claims)
        .setSubject(subject)
        .setIssuedAt(new Date(System.currentTimeMillis()))
        //Token valid for 2 minutes
        .setExpiration(new Date(System.currentTimeMillis()
            + 1000 * 60 * 2))
        .signWith(secretKey, SignatureAlgorithm.HS512)
        .compact();
```

```java
  }

  //Validate the token by checking username and expiry
  public Boolean validateToken(String token, String username) {
    final String extractedUsername = extractUsername(token);
    return (extractedUsername.equals(username)
        && !isTokenExpired(token));
  }

  public String generateRefreshToken(String username) {
    Map<String, Object> claims = new HashMap<>();
    //Just use the username for claims
    return createRefreshToken(claims, username);
  }

  public String createRefreshToken(Map<String, Object> claims,
                                   String subject) {
    Date expirationDate = new Date(System.currentTimeMillis()
        + 1000L * 60 * 60 * 24 * 30); //Use 'L' to avoid int overflow!

    return Jwts.builder()
        .setClaims(claims)
        .setSubject(subject)
        .setIssuedAt(new Date(System.currentTimeMillis()))
        .setExpiration(expirationDate) //Token valid for 30 days
        .signWith(secretKey, SignatureAlgorithm.HS512)
        .compact();
  }

  //Validate the refresh token
  public boolean validateRefreshToken(String token) {
    try {
      //Extract claims
      Claims claims = extractAllClaims(token);

      //Check if the token has expired
      if (claims.getExpiration().before(new Date())) {
        return false; //Token expired
      }
      //Token is valid
      return true;
    } catch (ExpiredJwtException e) {
      System.out.println("Token has expired: " + e.getMessage());
      return false;
    } catch (SignatureException e) {
      System.out.println("Invalid token signature: " + e.getMessage());
      return false;
    } catch (Exception e) {
      System.out.println("Invalid token: " + e.getMessage());
      return false;
    }
  }
}
```

LISTING 11-4: JwtUtilities.java

Note that we also change the token duration to 2 minutes. Also, make sure to use the L suffix in the calculation of the refresh token duration (1000L * 60 * 60 * 24 * 30). If you omit it then the calculation will take place with integers and the result will roll over to negative values.

Next, we should update the request filter so that it does not process the token refresh and revoke requests:

```
package com.example.Eshop.config;

import org.springframework.security.authentication.UsernamePasswordAuthenticationToken;
import org.springframework.security.core.context.SecurityContextHolder;
import org.springframework.security.core.userdetails.UserDetails;
import org.springframework.security.core.userdetails.UserDetailsService;
import org.springframework.security.web.authentication.WebAuthenticationDetailsSource;
import org.springframework.stereotype.Component;
import org.springframework.web.filter.OncePerRequestFilter;
import jakarta.servlet.FilterChain;
import jakarta.servlet.ServletException;
import jakarta.servlet.http.HttpServletRequest;
import jakarta.servlet.http.HttpServletResponse;
import java.io.IOException;

@Component
public class JwtRequestFilter extends OncePerRequestFilter {
  private final JwtUtilities jwtUtil;
  private final UserDetailsService myUserDetailsService;

  public JwtRequestFilter(JwtUtilities jwtUtil,
                    UserDetailsService myUserDetailsService) {
    this.jwtUtil = jwtUtil;
    this.myUserDetailsService = myUserDetailsService;
  }

  @Override
  protected void doFilterInternal(HttpServletRequest request,
                            HttpServletResponse response,
                            FilterChain chain)
      throws ServletException, IOException {

    //Skip filtering for login endpoint
    String path = request.getServletPath();
    if (path.equals("/auth/login")
        || path.equals("/auth/refresh")
        || path.equals("/auth/revoke")) {
      chain.doFilter(request, response);
      return;
    }

    final String authorizationHeader = request.getHeader("Authorization");
```

```
    String username = null;
    String jwt = null;

    // Extract JWT from the Authorization header (if present)
    if (authorizationHeader != null
        && authorizationHeader.startsWith("Bearer ")) {
      jwt = authorizationHeader.substring(7); //Remove "Bearer " prefix

      try {
        username = jwtUtil.extractUsername(jwt);

        // Check if the token is expired
        if (jwtUtil.isTokenExpired(jwt)) {
          //Return 401 Unauthorized
          response.setStatus(HttpServletResponse.SC_UNAUTHORIZED);
          response.getWriter().write("Token is expired");
          return;
        }
      } catch (Exception e) {
        //If an error occurs during token processing, return 401
        response.setStatus(HttpServletResponse.SC_UNAUTHORIZED);
        response.getWriter().write("Invalid token");
        return;
      }
    }

    //Validate the token and set authentication
    if (username != null
        && SecurityContextHolder.getContext().getAuthentication() == null) {
      UserDetails userDetails
          = this.myUserDetailsService.loadUserByUsername(username);

      if (jwtUtil.validateToken(jwt, userDetails.getUsername())) {
        UsernamePasswordAuthenticationToken authToken
            = new UsernamePasswordAuthenticationToken(
                userDetails, null, userDetails.getAuthorities());
        authToken.setDetails(new
WebAuthenticationDetailsSource().buildDetails(request));
        SecurityContextHolder.getContext().setAuthentication(authToken);
      }
    }

    chain.doFilter(request, response);
  }
}
```
LISTING 11-5: JwtRequestFilter.java

Frontend

On the Angular side, we start with updating the User model to reflect the changes in the backend:

```
export class User {
  id?: number;
  username?: string;
  password?: string;
  firstName?: string;
  lastName?: string;
  token?: string;
  refreshToken?: string;
  refreshTokenExpiry?: Date;
  role?: string;
  email?: string;
}
```

LISTING 11-6: user.ts

The bulk of our work takes place in th JWT interceptor class:

```
import { Injectable } from "@angular/core";
import { HttpEvent, HttpHandler, HttpInterceptor, HttpRequest }
  from "@angular/common/http";
import { BehaviorSubject, Observable, catchError, filter, switchMap, take,
throwError } from "rxjs";
import { environment } from "../../environments/environment";
import { StoreService } from "../services/store.service";
import { Router } from "@angular/router";
import { AuthenticationService } from "../services/authentication.service";
import { User } from "../models/user";

@Injectable()
export class JwtInterceptor implements HttpInterceptor {

  private isRefreshing = false;
  private refreshTokenSubject: BehaviorSubject<string | null>
    = new BehaviorSubject<string | null>(null);

  constructor(private router: Router,
    private storeService: StoreService,
    private authenticationService: AuthenticationService) { }

  intercept(request: HttpRequest<any>, next: HttpHandler):
    Observable<HttpEvent<any>> {

    const currentUser = this.storeService.user;
    const isLoggedIn = currentUser && currentUser.token;
    const isApiUrl = request.url.startsWith(environment.apiUrl);
    if (isLoggedIn && isApiUrl) {

      request = request.clone({
        setHeaders: {
          Authorization: `Bearer ${currentUser?.token}`
        }
      });
```

```typescript
    return next.handle(request).pipe(
      catchError(error => {
        // If 401 Unauthorized error, try to refresh the token
        if (error.status === 401 && !this.isRefreshing) {
          return this.handle401Error(request, next);
        }
        return throwError(() => error);
      })
    );
  }
  return next.handle(request);
}

private handle401Error(request: HttpRequest<any>, next: HttpHandler)
  : Observable<HttpEvent<any>> {
  const currentUser = this.storeService.user;
  if (!this.isRefreshing) {
    this.isRefreshing = true;
    this.refreshTokenSubject.next(null);

    return this.authenticationService.refreshToken(currentUser?.token || '',
      currentUser?.refreshToken || '').pipe(
        switchMap((newUser: User) => {
          this.isRefreshing = false;
          this.refreshTokenSubject.next(newUser.token || '');
          return next.handle(request = request.clone({
            setHeaders: {
              Authorization: `Bearer ${newUser?.token}`
            }
          }));
        }),
        catchError((err) => {
          this.isRefreshing = false;
          this.authenticationService.logout(currentUser?.refreshToken || '');
          return throwError(() => err);
        })
      );
  } else {
    return this.refreshTokenSubject.pipe(
      filter(token => token !== null),
      take(1),
      switchMap(token => {
        return next.handle(request = request.clone({
          setHeaders: {
            Authorization: `Bearer ${currentUser?.token}`
          }
        }));
      })
    );
  }
}
}
```

LISTING 10-7: *jwt.interceptor.ts*

The interceptor again adds the current token to every outgoing request. However, when it receives a 401 response from the backend, it will initiate the token refresh process. If a refresh is already in progress, subsequent requests will wait until the refresh completes.

The `isRefreshing` flag ensures that only one refresh request is sent, and the `refreshTokenSubject` helps other requests wait until the new token is available.

When the new token is received, then the failed request will be re-sent with the correct token.

In the `AuthenticationService` class, the corresponding `refreshToken()` function sends a POST request (`/auth/refresh`) to the API. This request contains the current access and refresh tokens:

```
import { HttpClient } from '@angular/common/http';
import { Injectable } from '@angular/core';
import { map } from 'rxjs/operators';
import { environment } from '../../environments/environment';
import { User } from '../models/user';
import { StoreService } from './store.service';

@Injectable({
  providedIn: 'root'
})
export class AuthenticationService {

  constructor(
    public storeService: StoreService,
    private http: HttpClient
  ) { }

  login(username: string, password: string) {
    return this.http.post<User>(`${environment.apiUrl}/auth/login`,
      { username, password })
      .pipe(
        map(user => {
          sessionStorage.setItem('user', JSON.stringify(user));
          this.storeService.user = user;
          return user;
        })
      );
  }

  logout(refreshToken: string) {
    this.http.post<any>(`${environment.apiUrl}/auth/revoke`,
      { refreshToken })
      .subscribe();

    this.storeService.cart.emptyCart();
    sessionStorage.removeItem('user');

    this.storeService.user = null;
```

```
  }

  refreshToken(token: string, refreshToken: string) {
    return this.http.post<User>(`${environment.apiUrl}/auth/refresh`,
      { token, refreshToken })
      .pipe(
        map(user => {
          sessionStorage.setItem('user', JSON.stringify(user));
          this.storeService.user = user;
          return user;
        })
      );
  }
}
```

LISTING 10-8: authentication.service.ts

You may also note here, that the logout() function has been modified. Apart from removing the current user from session storage, it also sends a POST request (/auth/revoke) to the API. This function is called from AppComponent class when the user clicks on Log out:

```
import { Component } from '@angular/core';
import { StoreService } from './services/store.service';
import { AuthenticationService } from './services/authentication.service';
import { Router } from '@angular/router';
import { User } from './models/user';

@Component({
  selector: 'app-root',
  templateUrl: './app.component.html',
  styleUrls: ['./app.component.css']
})
export class AppComponent {

  user: User | null = null;

  constructor(
    private router: Router,
    public authenticationService: AuthenticationService,
    public storeService: StoreService
  ) {
    this.storeService.user$.subscribe(x => this.user = x);
  }

  logout(e: Event) {
    e.preventDefault();
    const currentUser = this.storeService.user;
    this.authenticationService.logout(currentUser?.refreshToken || '');
    this.router.navigate(['/login']);
  }
}
```

LISTING 10-9: app.component.ts

Now, the access token expires every 2 minutes. When the user tries to access a protected route, the token is refreshed automatically for 2 more minutes, keeping the user logged in.

You may find the code for this chapter here:

https://github.com/htset/htset-eshop-angular-18-spring/tree/part10

11. Checkout

In this chapter, we will implement the first part of the checkout functionality. In this page, the customer gets a summary of the selected items in the cart and enters the delivery address. The user may add a new address, or select a previously selected one, that has been stored in the database during a previous purchase.

Here, we will see how to use *signals* in our code as well as how to make a component that is used by another component, and how those two components interact. Furthermore, we will see again how to create reactive forms in our components.

Frontend

Let's start with the introduction of the `Address` model:

```typescript
export interface Address {
  id: number;
  userId: number
  firstName: string;
  lastName: string;
  street: string;
  zip: string;
  city: string;
  country: string;
}
```

LISTING 11-1: address.ts

Next, we create the delivery-address component that will enable users to select an existing delivery address or create a new one. Users will also be able to modify an existing address or delete it altogether.

The new component is created in the `shared` folder, as it a general-purpose component that may be used also in other contexts:

```html
<form [formGroup]="addressForm" (ngSubmit)="onSubmit()">
  <div class="form-group">
    <label for="firstname">First Name:</label>
    <input type="text"
           class="form-control form-control-sm" formControlName="firstName" />
  </div>
  <div class="form-group">
    <label for="lastname">Last Name:</label>
    <input type="text"
           class="form-control form-control-sm" formControlName="lastName" />
  </div>
  <div class="form-group">
    <label for="street">Street:</label>
    <input type="text"
```

```html
          class="form-control form-control-sm" formControlName="street" />
    </div>
    <div class="form-group">
      <label for="zip">ZIP code:</label>
      <input type="text"
             class="form-control form-control-sm" formControlName="zip" />
    </div>
    <div class="form-group">
      <label for="city">City:</label>
      <input type="text"
             class="form-control form-control-sm" formControlName="city" />
    </div>
    <div class="form-group">
      <label for="country">Country:</label>
      <input type="text"
             class="form-control form-control-sm" formControlName="country" />
    </div>
    <button type="submit"
            class="btn btn-primary" [disabled]="!addressForm.valid">
      Save
    </button>
</form>
```

LISTING 11-2: delivery-address.component.html

The delivery-address component consists of a reactive form. The form is controlled by the `addressForm` form group. This form group contains a number of form controls that correspond to the text inputs presented in the template:

```typescript
import { Component, OnInit, model } from '@angular/core';
import { Address } from '../../../models/address';
import { FormControl, FormGroup, Validators } from '@angular/forms';

@Component({
  selector: 'app-delivery-address',
  templateUrl: './delivery-address.component.html',
  styleUrl: './delivery-address.component.css'
})
export class DeliveryAddressComponent implements OnInit {

  address = model<Address>();

  addressForm = new FormGroup({
    firstName: new FormControl('', Validators.required),
    lastName: new FormControl('', Validators.required),
    street: new FormControl('', Validators.required),
    zip: new FormControl('', Validators.required),
    city: new FormControl('', Validators.required),
    country: new FormControl('', Validators.required),
    id: new FormControl(''),
    userId: new FormControl('')
  });
```

```
  constructor() { }

  ngOnInit(): void {
    if (this.address !== undefined) {
      this.addressForm.controls
        .firstName.setValue(this.address()?.firstName || '');
      this.addressForm.controls
        .lastName.setValue(this.address()?.lastName || '');
      this.addressForm.controls
        .street.setValue(this.address()?.street || '');
      this.addressForm.controls
        .zip.setValue(this.address()?.zip || '');
      this.addressForm.controls
        .city.setValue(this.address()?.city || '');
      this.addressForm.controls
        .country.setValue(this.address()?.country || '');
      this.addressForm.controls
        .id.setValue(this.address()?.id.toString() || '0');
      this.addressForm.controls.
        userId.setValue(this.address()?.userId.toString() || '0');
    }
  }

  onSubmit() {
    var addr: Address = {
      firstName: this.addressForm.value.firstName || '',
      lastName: this.addressForm.value.lastName || '',
      street: this.addressForm.value.street || '',
      zip: this.addressForm.value.zip || '',
      city: this.addressForm.value.city || '',
      country: this.addressForm.value.country || '',
      id: parseInt(this.addressForm.value.id || '0'),
      userId: parseInt(this.addressForm.value.userId || '0')
    }

    this.address.set(addr);
  }
}
```

LISTING 11-3: delivery-address.component.ts

In reactive forms, the form model is the source of truth. This means that the form controls contain the information about the delivery address, and that they provide this information to the input boxes, through the `formControl` directive.

The delivery-address component will be inserted into another component that we will create next, the *checkout* component. The host component informs the child component of a preselected address to be displayed, by using a `model` signal.

In turn, after we submit the form, the child component informs the host component of the new address, by emitting an event. This event can be captured in the parent component by listening for an event whose name is the name of the model variable suffixed by "Change". In our case, the name of the event is addressChange.

Let's now create the checkout component:

```
<h2>Checkout</h2>

@if(storeService.cart.cartItems.length > 0){
<div class="card">
  <div class="card-body" id="cartBody">
    <h3 class="card-header">Cart</h3>
    <table class="table table-striped">
      <tr>
        <th>Item name</th>
        <th>Quantity</th>
        <th>Unit Price</th>
        <th>Total Price</th>
      </tr>
      @for(ci of storeService.cart.cartItems; track ci){
      <tr>
        <td>{{ci.item.name}}</td>
        <td>{{ci.quantity}}</td>
        <td>{{ci.item.price}}</td>
        <td>{{ci.item.price * ci.quantity}}</td>
      </tr>
      }
    </table>
    Cart Total: {{storeService.cart.getTotalValue()}}
  </div>
</div>
}

@if(storeService.cart.cartItems.length == 0){
<div class="card">
  <div class="card-body" id="noCartBody">
    <h3 class="card-header">Cart</h3>
    Cart is empty
  </div>
</div>
}

@if(storeService.user?.id){
<div class="card">
  <div class="card-body" id="addressBody">
    <h3 class="card-header">Delivery Address</h3>
    <form (ngSubmit)="onSubmit()">
      <table style="width:100%;">
        @for(addr of addressList(); track addr){
        <tr>
          <td style="vertical-align: top;">
            <input type="radio"
                   id="selectedAddress{{addr.id}}"
                   name="selectedAddress"
                   [value]="addr.id"
                   [ngModel]="selectedAddressId()"
```

```
              (change)="selectionChanged($any($event.target).id)"/>
    </td>

    @if(addressIdForModification() != addr.id){
    <td>
      <strong>{{addr.firstName + ' ' + addr.lastName}}</strong><br />
      {{addr.street}} <br />
      {{addr.zip + ' ' + addr.city}}<br />
      {{addr.country}} <br />
    </td>
    }

    @if(addressIdForModification() == addr.id){
    <td>
      <app-delivery-address
        (addressChange)="addressChanged($event)"
        [address]="addr">
      </app-delivery-address>
    </td>
    }

    <td style="vertical-align: top;">
      @if(addressIdForModification() != addr.id){
      <button type="button"
              id="modify{{addr.id}}"
              (click)="modifyAddress(addr)">
        Modify
      </button>
      }

      @if(addressIdForModification() == addr.id){
      <button type="button"
              id="cancel{{addr.id}}"
              (click)="cancelModifyAddress()">
        Cancel
      </button>
      }

      <br />
      @if(addressIdForModification() != addr.id){
      <button type="button"
              (click)="deleteAddress(addr)">
        Delete
      </button>
      }
    </td>
</tr>
}
<tr>
  <td style="vertical-align: top;">
    <input type="radio"
           id="selectedAddress0"
           name="selectedAddress"
           [value]="0"
           [ngModel]="selectedAddressId()"
```

```
                        (change)="selectionChanged($any($event.target).id)"/>
          </td>
          <td>
            <strong>New address:</strong><br />
            @if(selectedAddressId() == 0){
            <app-delivery-address
              (addressChange)="addressChanged($event)">
            </app-delivery-address>
            }
          </td>
        </tr>
      </table>
      <input type="submit"
             id="toPayment"
             [disabled]="!((addressIdForModification()      ==      -1)     &&
(selectedAddressId() > 0) && (storeService.cart.cartItems.length > 0))"
             value="To payment" />
    </form>
  </div>
</div>
}

@if(!storeService.user?.id){
  <div class="card">
    <div class="card-body" id="loginLink">
      <h3 class="card-header">Delivery Address</h3>
      <p>
        You need to <a [routerLink]="['/login']"
                        [queryParams]="{returnUrl: 'checkout'}">log in</a>
      </p>
    </div>
  </div>
}

<button routerLink="/cart">Back to Cart</button>
<br />
```

LISTING 11-4: checkout.component.html

The template can be divided in two parts. On the top half, a summary of the shopping cart contents is provided.

On the bottom half (and only if the customer has logged in), we display (using an @for loop) the already available delivery addresses for the current user, as retrieved from the database. We also provide the option for the user to insert a new address. In both cases, we use the *delivery-address* component, and we pass as parameters the event handler for the addressChange and the address to be used for display each time (this will be assigned to the model signal in the child component).

The user is also able to modify a selected delivery address, as well as delete the address from the database. Here is the code for the component:

```typescript
import { Component, OnInit, signal } from '@angular/core';
import { Address } from '../../../models/address';
import { StoreService } from '../../../services/store.service';
import { UserService } from '../../../services/user.service';
import { Router } from '@angular/router';
import { mergeMap, tap } from 'rxjs';

@Component({
  selector: 'app-checkout',
  templateUrl: './checkout.component.html',
  styleUrl: './checkout.component.css'
})
export class CheckoutComponent implements OnInit {

  addressIdForModification = signal<number>(-1);
  selectedAddressId = signal<number>(-1);
  addressList = signal<Address[]>([]);

  constructor(public storeService: StoreService,
    public userService: UserService,
    public router: Router) { }

  ngOnInit(): void {
    if (this?.storeService?.user?.id || 0 > 0) {
      //get addresses already saved by user
      this.userService
        .getAddressByUserId(this?.storeService?.user?.id || 0)
        .subscribe(addresses => {
          this.addressList.set(addresses);
          this.selectedAddressId.set(this.storeService.deliveryAddress);
        })
    }
  }

  selectionChanged(elementId: string): void {
    //elementId contains the ID of the selected address
    this.selectedAddressId.set(parseInt(elementId.
      substring(15, elementId.length)));
  }

  //function that is passed to the DeliveryAddress component
  addressChanged(addr: Address | undefined): void {
    let newAddress: Address;
    if (addr !== undefined) {
      addr.userId = this?.storeService?.user?.id || 0;

      if (this?.storeService?.user?.id || 0 > 0) {
        //save address in DB
        this.userService.saveAddress(addr).pipe(
          tap(res => newAddress = res),
          mergeMap(res => this.userService
            .getAddressByUserId(this?.storeService?.user?.id || 0))
        )
          .subscribe(addresses => {
            this.addressList.set(addresses);
```

```
            //change selected checkbox
            this.selectedAddressId.set(newAddress.id || 0);
            //toggle modifying
            this.addressIdForModification.set(-1);
          })
      }
    }
  }

  modifyAddress(addr: Address): void {
    this.addressIdForModification.set(addr.id || -1);
  }

  cancelModifyAddress(): void {
    this.addressIdForModification.set(-1);
  }

  deleteAddress(addr: Address): void {
    if (this?.storeService?.user?.id || 0 > 0) {
      this.userService.deleteAddress(addr.id)
        .subscribe(addressId => {
          this.addressList.set(this.addressList()
            ?.filter(addr => addr.id != addressId));

          if (this.selectedAddressId() == addressId)
            this.selectedAddressId.set(-1);
        })
    }
  }

  onSubmit(): void {
    this.storeService.deliveryAddress = this.selectedAddressId();
    this.router.navigate(['/payment']);
  }
}
```

LISTING 11-5: checkout.component.ts

The most interesting part of this code is the event handler addressChanged(). Here, we use mergeMap to run the saveAddress and getAddressByUserId operations in sequence, and to avoid placing one subscribe method into the other.

Note also that we are using 3 signals for our class members instead of JavaScript properties. Also note in the template, how we bind such a signal to an input:

```
<input type="radio"
  id="selectedAddress{{addr.id}}"
  name="selectedAddress"
  [value]="addr.id"
  [ngModel]="selectedAddressId()"
  (change)="selectionChanged($any($event.target).id)"/>
```

LISTING 11-6: checkout.component.html

The checkout component makes use of address-handling functions defined in `UserService`. Those functions make HTTP calls to the backend API:

```typescript
import { HttpClient, HttpHeaders } from '@angular/common/http';
import { Injectable } from '@angular/core';
import { User } from '../models/user';
import { environment } from '../../environments/environment';
import { Address } from '../models/address';

@Injectable({
  providedIn: 'root'
})
export class UserService {

  httpOptions = {
    headers: new HttpHeaders({ 'Content-Type': 'application/json' })
  };

  constructor(private http: HttpClient) { }

  getAllUsers() {
    return this.http.get<User[]>(`${environment.apiUrl}/users`);
  }

  getAddressByUserId(userId: number) {
    return this.http.get<Address[]>(`${environment.apiUrl}/addresses/${userId}`);
  }

  saveAddress(address: Address) {
    return this.http.post<Address>(`${environment.apiUrl}/address`, address);
  }

  deleteAddress(addressId?: number) {
    return this.http.delete<number>(`${environment.apiUrl}/address/${addressId}`);
  }
}
```

LISTING 11-7: user.service.ts

Note also that we have added the currently selected delivery address ID into `StoreService`:

```typescript
...
  private readonly _deliveryAddress = new BehaviorSubject<number>(-1);
  readonly deliveryAddress$ = this._deliveryAddress.asObservable();

  get deliveryAddress(): number {
    return this._deliveryAddress.getValue();
  }
```

```
set deliveryAddress(val: number) {
  this._deliveryAddress.next(val);
}
...
```

LISTING 11-8: store.service.ts

Finally, we need a routing entry in *app-routing.module.ts*, so that we can navigate from the cart to the checkout component:

```
...
const routes: Routes = [
  { path: '', component: ItemsComponent },
  { path: 'items', component: ItemsComponent },
  { path: 'items/:id', component: ItemDetailsComponent },
  { path: 'cart', component: CartComponent },
  { path: 'checkout', component: CheckoutComponent, canActivate: [AuthGuard] },
  { path: 'login', component: LoginComponent },
  {
    path: 'admin', component: AdminHomeComponent,
    canActivate: [AuthGuard],
    children: [
      {
        path: 'users', component: AdminUsersComponent,
        canActivate: [AuthGuard]
      }
    ]
  },
];
...
```

LISTING 11-9: app-routing.module.ts

Note that we will need to authenticate first, in order to proceed with the checkout route.

Finally, we make a small addition to the *auth.guard.ts* file:

```
import { Injectable } from "@angular/core";
import { ActivatedRouteSnapshot, CanActivate, Router, RouterStateSnapshot }
  from "@angular/router";
import { StoreService } from "../services/store.service";
import { AuthenticationService } from "../services/authentication.service";
import { lastValueFrom } from "rxjs";

@Injectable({ providedIn: 'root' })
export class AuthGuard implements CanActivate {
  constructor(
    private router: Router,
    private storeService: StoreService,
    private authenticationService: AuthenticationService
  ) { }
```

```
  canActivate(route: ActivatedRouteSnapshot,
    state: RouterStateSnapshot) {
    const currentUser = this.storeService.user;
    if (currentUser && currentUser.role == 'ADMIN') {
      return true;
    }
    else if (currentUser && currentUser.role == 'CUSTOMER') {
      if (route.url.some(segment => segment.path.includes('admin'))) {
        this.router.navigate(['/items']);
      }
      return true;
    }

    this.router.navigate(['/login'],
      { queryParams: { returnUrl: state.url } });
    return false;
  }
}
```

LISTING 11-10: auth.guard.ts

We made this change to differentiate between customer router and admin routes, that both require logging in.

Backend

Let's move now to the backend API project. First, we introduce the model for the delivery address:

```
package com.example.Eshop.models;

import jakarta.persistence.Entity;
import jakarta.persistence.GeneratedValue;
import jakarta.persistence.GenerationType;
import jakarta.persistence.Id;
import lombok.Data;

@Entity
@Data
public class Address {
  @Id
  @GeneratedValue(strategy = GenerationType.IDENTITY)
  public Long id;
  public Long userId;
  public String firstName;
  public String lastName;
  public String street;
  public String zip;
  public String city;
```

```
    public String country;
}
```

LISTING 11-11: Address.java

Next, we create a new Web API controller, `AddressController` that contains CRUD functionality for the handling of delivery addresses:

```
package com.example.Eshop.controllers;

import com.example.Eshop.models.Address;
import com.example.Eshop.services.AddressService;
import org.springframework.http.ResponseEntity;
import org.springframework.web.bind.annotation.*;
import java.util.List;

@RestController
@RequestMapping("/addresses")
public class AddressController {

  private AddressService addressService;
  public AddressController(AddressService addressService){
    this.addressService = addressService;
  }

  @GetMapping("/{userId}")
  public ResponseEntity<List<Address>> getAddressesByUserId(@PathVariable Long userId) {
    List<Address> addresses = addressService.getAddressesByUserId(userId);
    return ResponseEntity.ok(addresses);
  }

  @PostMapping
  public ResponseEntity<Address> saveAddress(@RequestBody Address address) {
    try {
      Address savedAddress;
      if (address.getId() > 0) {
        savedAddress = addressService.saveAddress(address);
        //Return 200 OK if it's an update
        return ResponseEntity.ok(savedAddress);
      } else {
        address.setId(null);
        savedAddress = addressService.saveAddress(address);
        //Return 201 Created if it's new
        return ResponseEntity.status(201).body(savedAddress);
      }
    } catch (RuntimeException e) {
      //Return 404 if address to update is not found
      return ResponseEntity.notFound().build();
    }
  }

  @DeleteMapping("/{id}")
```

```java
  public ResponseEntity<Void> deleteAddress(@PathVariable Long id) {
    try {
      addressService.deleteAddress(id);
      //Return 204 No Content on successful delete
      return ResponseEntity.noContent().build();
    } catch (RuntimeException e) {
      //Return 404 Not Found if address does not exist
      return ResponseEntity.notFound().build();
    }
  }
}
```

LISTING 11-12: AddressController.java

We also add the corresponding service:

```
package com.example.Eshop.services;

import com.example.Eshop.models.Address;
import com.example.Eshop.repositories.AddressRepository;
import org.springframework.stereotype.Service;
import java.util.List;
import java.util.Optional;
import java.util.List;
import java.util.Optional;

@Service
public class AddressService {

  private AddressRepository addressRepository;

  public AddressService(AddressRepository addressRepository){
    this.addressRepository = addressRepository;
  }

  public List<Address> getAddressesByUserId(Long userId) {
    return addressRepository.findByUserId(userId);
  }

  public Address saveAddress(Address address) {
    //Check if the address has an ID (indicating an update)
    if (address.getId() > 0) {
      //Get the existing address from the database
      Optional<Address> optionalAddress
          = addressRepository.findById(address.getId());

      if (optionalAddress.isPresent()) {
        //Update the existing address
        Address existingAddress = optionalAddress.get();
        existingAddress.setFirstName(address.getFirstName());
        existingAddress.setLastName(address.getLastName());
        existingAddress.setStreet(address.getStreet());
        existingAddress.setZip(address.getZip());
```

```
            existingAddress.setCity(address.getCity());
            existingAddress.setCountry(address.getCountry());

            //Save and return the updated address
            return addressRepository.save(existingAddress);
        } else {
            throw new RuntimeException("Address not found with id: "
                + address.getId());
        }
    } else {
        //If no ID is present, it's a new address, so save it
        return addressRepository.save(address);
    }
}

public void deleteAddress(Long id) {
    //Check if the address exists before attempting to delete
    if (addressRepository.existsById(id)) {
        addressRepository.deleteById(id);
    } else {
        throw new RuntimeException("Address not found with id: " + id);
    }
  }
}
```

LISTING 11-13: AddressService.java

Finally, we add the repository for the address handling:

```
package com.example.Eshop.repositories;

import com.example.Eshop.models.Address;
import org.springframework.data.jpa.repository.JpaRepository;

import java.util.List;
import java.util.Optional;

public interface AddressRepository extends JpaRepository<Address, Long> {
  List<Address> findByUserId(Long userId);
}
```

LISTING 11-14: AddressRepository.java

In the next chapter, we will continue with the payment and order placing functionality. You may find the code for this chapter here:

https://github.com/htset/htset-eshop-angular-18-spring/tree/part11

12. Order validation and submission

In the previous chapter, we created the checkout page, where the customer views a summary of the cart and selects the delivery address. Here, we will finish the checkout process by submitting the order to the backend. We will also see how to perform validation, both on the frontend and the backend.

Frontend

We start by creating the models that we will use for the order submission. We define the `Order`, `OrderDetail` and `CreditCard` classes:

```
export class OrderDetail {
  public id?: number;
  public orderId?: number;
  public itemId?: number;
  public itemName?: string;
  public itemUnitPrice?: number;
  public quantity?: number;
  public totalPrice?: number;
}
```

LISTING 12-1: orderDetail.ts

```
export class CreditCard {
  cardNumber?: string;
  holderName?: string;
  code?: string;
  expiryMonth?: number;
  expiryYear?: number;
}
```

LISTING 12-2: creditCard.ts

```
import { CreditCard } from "./creditCard";
import { OrderDetail } from "./orderDetail";

export class Order {
  public id?: number;
  public userId?: number;
  public orderDate?: Date;
  public orderDetails?: OrderDetail[];
  public totalPrice?: number;
  public creditCard?: CreditCard;
  public deliveryAddressId?: number;
  public firstName?: string;
  public lastName?: string;
  public street?: string;
  public zip?: string;
```

```
  public city?: string;
  public country?: string;
}
```

LISTING 12-3: order.ts

Next, we create a new component (payment) that will be the next page in the process of checkout. In this component, after the customer enters their credit card details and presses on *Finalize Order*, the order is submitted to the backend.

The payment component consists of a reactive form that is controlled in the component by a `FormGroup` object. During the definition of the `FormGroup`, we can select validation options on each of the associated `FormControl` objects.

```
import { Component, Input, OnInit } from '@angular/core';
import { AbstractControl, FormControl, FormGroup, Validators }
  from '@angular/forms';
import { Router } from '@angular/router';
import { Cart } from '../../../../app/models/cart';
import { Order } from '../../../../app/models/order';
import { OrderDetail } from '../../../../app/models/orderDetail';
import { OrderService } from '../../../../app/services/order.service';
import { StoreService } from '../../../../app/services/store.service';

@Component({
  selector: 'app-payment',
  templateUrl: './payment.component.html',
  styleUrls: ['./payment.component.css']
})
export class PaymentComponent implements OnInit {
  currentYear:number = new Date().getFullYear();

  paymentForm = new FormGroup({
    cardNumber: new FormControl('',
      [Validators.required, Validators.pattern(/^[0-9]{16}$/)]),
    holderName: new FormControl('',
      Validators.required),
    code: new FormControl('',
      [Validators.required, Validators.pattern(/^[0-9]{3}$/)]),
    expiryMonth: new FormControl('',
      Validators.required),
    expiryYear: new FormControl('',
      Validators.required)
  }, [ValidateExpirationDate]);

  constructor(public storeService: StoreService,
    private orderService: OrderService,
    private router: Router) { }

  ngOnInit(): void { }

  onSubmit(): void {
```

```typescript
    let userId = this?.storeService?.user?.id || 0;
    if (userId > 0) {
      //if user is logged in
      let order: Order = new Order();
      order.userId = userId;
      order.orderDetails = this.storeService
        .cart.cartItems
        .map(
          (cartItem) => {
            let orderDetail: OrderDetail = new OrderDetail();
            orderDetail.itemId = cartItem.item.id;
            orderDetail.quantity = cartItem.quantity;
            return orderDetail;
          });
      order.deliveryAddressId = this.storeService.deliveryAddress;
      order.creditCard = {
        cardNumber:
          this.paymentForm.controls.cardNumber.value || '',
        holderName:
          this.paymentForm.controls.holderName.value || '',
        code:
          this.paymentForm.controls.code.value || '',
        expiryMonth:
          parseInt(this.paymentForm.controls.expiryMonth.value || '0'),
        expiryYear:
          parseInt(this.paymentForm.controls.expiryYear.value || '0'),
    };

      //Submit order
      this.orderService.addOrder(order)
        .subscribe((orderResult: Order) => {
          this.storeService.order = orderResult;
          this.storeService.cart = new Cart();
          this.storeService.deliveryAddress = -1;

          this.router.navigate(['/summary']);
        })
    }
  }

  //creates a sequence of months
  numSequence(n: number): Array<number> {
    return Array(n);
  }

  //creates a sequence of years
  numSequenceStart(n: number, startFrom: number): number[] {
    return [...Array(n).keys()].map(i => i + startFrom);
  }
}

//Custom validator for the expiration date
function ValidateExpirationDate(control: AbstractControl)
  : { [key: string]: any } | null {
  if (control?.get("expiryMonth")?.value && control?.get("expiryYear")?.value) {
```

```
    let month: number = parseInt(control?.get("expiryMonth")?.value);
    let year: number = parseInt(control?.get("expiryYear")?.value);
    let currentDate = new Date();
    if (year < currentDate.getFullYear())
      return { 'CreditCardExpired': true };
    else if (year == currentDate.getFullYear()
        && month - 1 < currentDate.getMonth())
      return { 'CreditCardExpired': true };
  }
  return null;
}
```

LISTING 12-4: payment.component.ts

Apart from the Validators.required option for all controls, we use a regex pattern validation for the Card Number and CVV code text boxes. In this way, we can assure that they consist of 16 and 3 numbers respectively. Credit card validation is a very trivial one, as those numbers are in reality validated with the use of an algorithm.

There are libraries that we can use for this, but it is out of the scope of this book. In most cases anyway, we won't even need to add credit card details in our project; instead, we will redirect the customer to a specialized credit card processing page (e.g. from a bank).

Here we choose to deal with a more interesting case, the validation of more than one element on the same time. We have to ensure that the credit card has not expired; for that we need to write a custom validator function (validateExpirationDate) that accesses those two text boxes and checks them against the current month and year. This validator is not applied to either element, but on the form group instead.

On the template side, we have inserted suitable error messages under each element. The containing divs will appear when there is an error on the respective element, but only after the element has been touched or changed by the user. The submit button will become enabled when the whole formGroup passes validation:

```
<h2>Payment</h2>

@if(storeService.cart.cartItems.length > 0){
<div class="card">
  <div class="card-body" id="cartBody">
    <h3 class="card-header">Credit card details</h3>

    <form [formGroup]="paymentForm" (ngSubmit)="onSubmit()">
      <div class="form-row">
        <div class="form-group col-md-2">
          <label for="cardNumber">Credit card no.:</label>
          <input type="text" class="form-control form-control-sm"
              formControlName="cardNumber" />
          @if(paymentForm.controls['cardNumber'].invalid
            && (paymentForm.controls['cardNumber'].dirty
              || paymentForm.controls['cardNumber'].touched)){
```

```
        <div class="text-danger">
          @if(paymentForm.controls['cardNumber'].errors){
          <div>
            Please enter a valid credit card number
          </div>
          }
        </div>
        }
    </div>
</div>
<div class="form-row">
    <div class="form-group col-md-2">
      <label for="holderName">Holder's Name:</label>
      <input type="text" class="form-control form-control-sm"
             formControlName="holderName" />
      @if(paymentForm.controls['holderName'].invalid
        && (paymentForm.controls['holderName'].dirty
          || paymentForm.controls['holderName'].touched)){
      <div class="text-danger">
        @if(paymentForm.controls['holderName'].errors){
        <div>
          Please enter the card holder's name
        </div>
        }
      </div>
      }
    </div>
</div>
<div class="form-row">
    <div class="form-group col-md-2">
      <label for="code">CVV Code:</label>
      <input type="text" class="form-control form-control-sm"
             formControlName="code" />
      @if(paymentForm.controls['code'].invalid
        && (paymentForm.controls['code'].dirty
          || paymentForm.controls['code'].touched)){
      <div class="text-danger">
        @if(paymentForm.controls['code'].errors){
        <div>
          Please enter a valid CVV code
        </div>
        }
      </div>
      }
    </div>
</div>
<div class="form-row">
    <div class="form-group col-sm-1">
      <label for="expirydate">Expiry date:</label>
      <select formControlName="expiryMonth"
              class="form-control form-control-sm">
        @for(i of numSequence(12); track $index){
        <option [value]="$index+1">
          {{$index+1}}
        </option>
```

```
            }
          </select>
        </div>
        <div class="form-group col-sm-1">
          <label for="expirydate"> </label>
          <select formControlName="expiryYear"
                  class="form-control form-control-sm">
            @for(i of numSequenceStart(5, currentYear); track i){
            <option [value]="i">
              {{i}}
            </option>
            }
          </select>
        </div>
      </div>
      <div class="form-row">
        @if((paymentForm.controls['expiryMonth'].invalid
            || paymentForm.controls['expiryYear'].invalid)
          && (paymentForm.controls['expiryMonth'].dirty
            || paymentForm.controls['expiryMonth'].touched
            || paymentForm.controls['expiryYear'].dirty
            || paymentForm.controls['expiryYear'].touched)){
        <div class="text-danger">
          @if(paymentForm.controls['expiryMonth'].errors
            || paymentForm.controls['expiryYear'].errors){
          <div>
            Please enter the card's expiration date
          </div>
          }
        </div>
        }

        @if((paymentForm.invalid)
          && (paymentForm.controls['expiryMonth'].dirty
            || paymentForm.controls['expiryMonth'].touched
            || paymentForm.controls['expiryYear'].dirty
            || paymentForm.controls['expiryYear'].touched)){
        <div class="text-danger">
          @if(paymentForm.errors){
          <div>
            The credit card has expired
          </div>
          }
        </div>
        }
      </div>

      <button type="submit"
              [disabled]="!paymentForm.valid">
        Finalize Order
      </button>
    </form>
  </div>
</div>
```

```
}
@if(storeService.cart.cartItems.length == 0){
<div class="card">
  <div class="card-body" id="noCartBody">
    <h3 class="card-header">Cart</h3>
    Cart is empty
  </div>
</div>
}

<button routerLink="/checkout">Back to Checkout</button>
<br />
```

LISTING 12-5: payment.component.html

When submit is clicked and after all validations have passed, a new Order object is created. It is then filled with OrderDetail objects that correspond to the entries in the cart. The order is sent to the backend through the newly created OrderService:

```
import { HttpClient, HttpHeaders } from '@angular/common/http';
import { Injectable } from '@angular/core';
import { Order } from '../models/order';
import { environment } from '../../environments/environment';

@Injectable({
  providedIn: 'root'
})
export class OrderService {

  httpOptions = {
    headers: new HttpHeaders({ 'Content-Type': 'application/json' })
  };
  constructor(private http: HttpClient) { }

  addOrder(order: Order) {
    return this.http
      .post<Order>(`${environment.apiUrl}/orders`, order);
  }
}
```

LISTING 12-6: order.service.ts

If the submission is successful, we will be redirected to a new component, called Summary:

```
<p>Order successfully submitted</p>
<p>An email has been sent to: {{this.storeService.user?.email}}</p>
<p>Return to <a routerLink='/'>Items</a> page</p>
```

LISTING 12-7: summary.component.html

```
import { Component, OnInit } from '@angular/core';
import { StoreService } from '../../../services/store.service';
import { User } from '../../../models/user';


@Component({
  selector: 'app-summary',
  templateUrl: './summary.component.html',
  styleUrls: ['./summary.component.css']
})
export class SummaryComponent implements OnInit {

  public userInOrder?: User;
  constructor(public storeService: StoreService) { }

  ngOnInit(): void {
  }
}
```

LISTING 12-8: summary.component.ts

The returned Order object is stored in the StoreService object, for use in subsequent steps:

```
...
  private readonly _order = new BehaviorSubject<Order>(new Order());
  readonly order$ = this._order.asObservable();

  get order(): Order {
    return this._order.getValue();
  }

  set order(val: Order) {
    this._order.next(val);
  }
...
```

LISTING 12-9: store.service.ts

Finally, we should not forget to add the necessary routing entry into *app-routing.module.ts*:

```
...
  { path: 'payment', component: PaymentComponent, canActivate: [AuthGuard] },
  { path: 'summary', component: SummaryComponent, canActivate: [AuthGuard] },
...
```

LISTING 12-10: app-routing.module.ts

Backend

On the API side, we will first add a Maven dependency for validation functionality:

...

```xml
<dependency>
  <groupId>org.springframework.boot</groupId>
  <artifactId>spring-boot-starter-validation</artifactId>
</dependency>
...
```

LISTING 12-11: pom.xml

Next, we will create a new controller that will take care of the orders submission:

```java
package com.example.Eshop.controllers;

import com.example.Eshop.dtos.OrderDTO;
import com.example.Eshop.services.OrderService;
import org.springframework.http.HttpStatus;
import org.springframework.http.ResponseEntity;
import org.springframework.web.bind.annotation.*;
import jakarta.validation.Valid;

@RestController
@RequestMapping("/orders")
public class OrderController {

  private final OrderService orderService;

  public OrderController(OrderService orderService) {
    this.orderService = orderService;
  }

  @PostMapping
  public ResponseEntity<OrderDTO> postOrder(@Valid @RequestBody OrderDTO dto) {
    try {
      OrderDTO createdOrder = orderService.createOrder(dto);
      return ResponseEntity.status(HttpStatus.CREATED).body(createdOrder);
    } catch (Exception e) {
      return ResponseEntity.status(HttpStatus.BAD_REQUEST).build();
    }
  }
}
```

LISTING 12-12: OrderController.java

Here is the corresponding service used by the controller:

```java
package com.example.Eshop.services;

import com.example.Eshop.dtos.OrderDTO;
import com.example.Eshop.dtos.OrderDetailDTO;
import com.example.Eshop.models.Address;
import com.example.Eshop.models.Item;
import com.example.Eshop.models.Order;
import com.example.Eshop.models.OrderDetail;
```

```java
import com.example.Eshop.repositories.AddressRepository;
import com.example.Eshop.repositories.ItemRepository;
import com.example.Eshop.repositories.OrderRepository;
import org.springframework.stereotype.Service;
import jakarta.transaction.Transactional;
import java.math.BigDecimal;
import java.time.LocalDateTime;

@Service
public class OrderService {

    private final OrderRepository orderRepository;
    private final AddressRepository addressRepository;
    private final ItemRepository itemRepository;

    public OrderService(OrderRepository orderRepository,
                        AddressRepository addressRepository,
                        ItemRepository itemRepository) {
        this.orderRepository = orderRepository;
        this.addressRepository = addressRepository;
        this.itemRepository = itemRepository;
    }

    @Transactional
    public OrderDTO createOrder(OrderDTO dto) {
        Order newOrder = new Order();
        newOrder.setUserId(dto.getUserId());
        newOrder.setOrderDate(LocalDateTime.now());

        Address tempAddr = addressRepository.findById(dto.getDeliveryAddressId())
            .orElseThrow(() -> new RuntimeException("Address not found"));
        newOrder.setFirstName(tempAddr.getFirstName());
        newOrder.setLastName(tempAddr.getLastName());
        newOrder.setStreet(tempAddr.getStreet());
        newOrder.setZip(tempAddr.getZip());
        newOrder.setCity(tempAddr.getCity());
        newOrder.setCountry(tempAddr.getCountry());

        BigDecimal totalPrice = BigDecimal.ZERO;

        for (OrderDetailDTO detail : dto.getOrderDetails()) {
            Item tempItem = itemRepository.findById(detail.getItemId())
                .orElseThrow(() -> new RuntimeException("Item not found"));
            OrderDetail newOrderDetail = new OrderDetail();
            newOrderDetail.setItemId(detail.getItemId());
            newOrderDetail.setItemName(tempItem.getName());
            newOrderDetail.setItemUnitPrice(tempItem.getPrice());
            newOrderDetail.setQuantity(detail.getQuantity());
            newOrderDetail.setTotalPrice(tempItem.getPrice()
                .multiply(detail.getQuantity()));

            newOrderDetail.setOrder(newOrder);
            newOrder.getOrderDetails().add(newOrderDetail);
            totalPrice = totalPrice.add(newOrderDetail.getTotalPrice());
        }
```

```
      newOrder.setTotalPrice(totalPrice);
      orderRepository.save(newOrder);
      return createDTOFromOrder(newOrder);
    }

    private OrderDTO createDTOFromOrder(Order order) {
      OrderDTO dto = new OrderDTO();
      dto.setId(order.getId());
      dto.setUserId(order.getUserId());
      dto.setOrderDate(order.getOrderDate());

      dto.setTotalPrice(order.getTotalPrice());

      for (OrderDetail detail : order.getOrderDetails()) {
        OrderDetailDTO dtoDetail = new OrderDetailDTO();
        dtoDetail.setId(detail.getId());
        dtoDetail.setOrderId(detail.getOrder().getId());
        dtoDetail.setItemId(detail.getItemId());
        dtoDetail.setItemName(detail.getItemName());
        dtoDetail.setItemUnitPrice(detail.getItemUnitPrice());
        dtoDetail.setQuantity(detail.getQuantity());
        dtoDetail.setTotalPrice(detail.getTotalPrice());
        dto.getOrderDetails().add(dtoDetail);
      }

      return dto;
    }
}
```

LISTING 12-13: OrderService.java

The controller receives the submitted order in the form of a Data Transfer Object (DTO). At this point, it performs validation on the OrderDTO object (this is what the @Valid annotation does). We would like to be sure that all required information, such as delivery address and product details, is present in the OrderDTO object. If there is a problem with validation, we respond with response *400 Bad Request*.

Then the controller passes it to the service object. The service then uses the DTO to create the full Order object that will be eventually stored in the database.

Note that the frontend sends only the delivery address ID to the backend. The service then retrieves the address details from the database and stores them in the Order object. We choose to copy a snapshot of the delivery address, to avoid the case where this address entry is changed in the future. For the same reason we store also a snapshot of the information about each product, e.g. current price and description, as they may change too.

After the Order object (and the respective OrderDetails objects) are stored in the database, we create a new OrderDTO object that contains the resulting information, especially the new Order and OrderDetails IDs. This DTO is returned with the *201 Created* response.

We could use the same object for data transfer and data storage, and in simple applications this is the way to go. In more complex applications, it's better to have a DTO that will contain only the information that is exchanged between frontend and backend. Here, although this is not much of a complex web application, we opt to go with the DTO solution:

```
package com.example.Eshop.models;

import jakarta.persistence.*;
import jakarta.validation.constraints.*;
import lombok.Data;
import java.math.BigDecimal;
import java.time.LocalDateTime;
import java.util.ArrayList;
import java.util.List;

@Data
@Entity
@Table(name = "orders")
public class Order {
  @Id
  @GeneratedValue(strategy = GenerationType.IDENTITY)  // Auto-incremented ID
  @Column(nullable = false)
  private Long id;

  @NotNull
  @Column(nullable = false)
  private Long userId;

  @NotNull
  @Column(nullable = false)
  private LocalDateTime orderDate;

  @NotNull
  @Column(nullable = false, precision = 10, scale = 2)
  private BigDecimal totalPrice;

  @NotNull
  @OneToMany(mappedBy = "order", cascade = CascadeType.ALL)
  private List<OrderDetail> orderDetails;

  @NotBlank
  @Column(nullable = false)
  private String firstName;

  @NotBlank
  @Column(nullable = false)
  private String lastName;

  @NotBlank
  @Column(nullable = false)
  private String street;
```

```java
@NotBlank
@Column(nullable = false)
private String zip;

@NotBlank
@Column(nullable = false)
private String city;

@NotBlank
@Column(nullable = false)
private String country;


public Order(){
    orderDetails = new ArrayList<OrderDetail>();
}

@Override
public String toString() {
    return "Order{" +
        "id=" + id +
        ", userId=" + userId +
        ", orderDate=" + orderDate +
        ", totalPrice=" + totalPrice +
        ", firstName='" + firstName + '\'' +
        ", lastName='" + lastName + '\'' +
        ", street='" + street + '\'' +
        ", zip='" + zip + '\'' +
        ", city='" + city + '\'' +
        ", country='" + country + '\'' +
        '}';
    }
}
```

LISTING 12-14: Order.java

Two important notes here:

1. We use the annotation

```
@Table(name = "orders")
```

to change the name used for the orders table from *Order* to *Orders*. That's because *Order* is a keyword in SQL and will create errors.

2. We define our own `toString()` method to avoid a circular reference between the `Order` and `OrderDetail` entities, due to the way their `toString()` methods are implicitly called. This happens when one entity references another in a bidirectional relationship, and both try to include each other in their `toString()` methods, causing infinite recursion.

We can solve this issue by overriding the `toString()` method in our `Order` and `OrderDetail` classes to prevent the circular reference.

```
package com.example.Eshop.dtos;

import com.example.Eshop.validations.NotExpired;
import jakarta.validation.Valid;
import lombok.Data;
import jakarta.validation.constraints.*;
import java.math.BigDecimal;
import java.time.LocalDateTime;
import java.util.ArrayList;
import java.util.List;

@Data
@NotExpired //Use custom annotation
public class OrderDTO {

    private Long id;

    @NotNull
    private Long userId;

    private LocalDateTime orderDate;

    private BigDecimal totalPrice;

    @NotNull
    private List<OrderDetailDTO> orderDetails;

    @Valid
    private CreditCardDTO creditCard;

    @NotNull
    private Long deliveryAddressId;

    public OrderDTO(){
      orderDetails = new ArrayList<OrderDetailDTO>();
    }
}
```

LISTING 12-15: OrderDTO.cs

Note the `@Valid` annotation above the credit card property. This is used to trigger validation inside the the credit card object.

By comparing the two classes we can see that, for example, the `Order` class does not contain any credit card details, as we will avoid storing such information in our web application. The two classes also differ in their validation options. When receiving an `OrderDTO` in our backend, we expect it to contain the user ID, the order details, the delivery address ID selected and the credit card details. The rest of the fields will be used during the controller's response.

On the contrary, the Order class has defined everything as required, as we need all this information to be stored in the database.

Let's also see the other classes used:

```java
package com.example.Eshop.models;

import jakarta.persistence.*;
import jakarta.validation.constraints.*;
import lombok.Data;
import java.math.BigDecimal;

@Data
@Entity
public class OrderDetail {

  @Id
  @GeneratedValue(strategy = GenerationType.IDENTITY)
  @Column(nullable = false)
  private Long id;

  @ManyToOne
  @JoinColumn(name = "order_id", nullable = false)
  private Order order;

  @NotNull
  @Column(nullable = false)
  private Long itemId;

  @NotBlank
  @Column(nullable = false)
  private String itemName;

  @NotNull
  @DecimalMin(value = "0.0", inclusive = false)
  @Column(nullable = false, precision = 10, scale = 2)
  private BigDecimal itemUnitPrice;

  @NotNull
  @DecimalMin(value = "0.0", inclusive = false)
  @Column(nullable = false, precision = 10, scale = 2)
  private BigDecimal quantity;

  @NotNull
  @Column(nullable = false, precision = 10, scale = 2)
  private BigDecimal totalPrice;

  //Custom validation for Quantity > 0
  @AssertTrue(message = "Quantity must be greater than 0")
  public boolean isValidQuantity() {
    return quantity.compareTo(BigDecimal.ZERO) > 0;
  }
```

```java
    @Override
    public String toString() {
      return "OrderDetail{" +
          "id=" + id +
          ", itemId=" + itemId +
          ", itemName='" + itemName + '\'' +
          ", itemUnitPrice=" + itemUnitPrice +
          ", quantity=" + quantity +
          ", totalPrice=" + totalPrice +
          '}';
    }
}
```

LISTING 12-16: OrderDetail.java

```java
package com.example.Eshop.dtos;

import lombok.Data;
import jakarta.validation.constraints.*;
import java.math.BigDecimal;

@Data
public class OrderDetailDTO {

  private Long id;

  private Long orderId;

  @NotNull
  private Long itemId;

  private String itemName;

  @NotNull
  @DecimalMin(value = "0.0", inclusive = false)
  // Quantity must be greater than 0
  private BigDecimal quantity;

  private BigDecimal itemUnitPrice;

  private BigDecimal totalPrice;
}
```

LISTING 12-17: OrderDetailDTO.java

```java
package com.example.Eshop.dtos;

import jakarta.validation.constraints.*;
import lombok.Data;

import java.time.LocalDate;
```

```java
@Data
public class CreditCardDTO{

  @NotNull
  @Pattern(regexp = "^[0-9]{16}$", message = "Card number consists of 16 numbers")
  private String cardNumber;

  @NotNull
  private String holderName;

  @NotNull
  @Pattern(regexp = "^[0-9]{3}$", message = "CVV consists of 3 numbers")
  private String code;

  @NotNull
  @Min(1)
  @Max(12)
  private Integer expiryMonth;

  @NotNull
  private Integer expiryYear;

  //Validate if the card is expired
  public boolean isCardExpired() {
    LocalDate currentDate = LocalDate.now();
    LocalDate cardExpiryDate = LocalDate.of(expiryYear,
        expiryMonth, 1).withDayOfMonth(1);
    return currentDate.isAfter(cardExpiryDate);
  }
}
```

LISTING 12-18: CreditCardDTO.java

Next, we add a validation exception handler. If a validation fails, then this handler will kick in and will return a *400 Bad Request* response to the frontend:

```java
package com.example.Eshop.exceptions;

import org.springframework.http.HttpHeaders;
import org.springframework.http.HttpStatusCode;
import org.springframework.http.ResponseEntity;
import org.springframework.web.bind.MethodArgumentNotValidException;
import org.springframework.web.context.request.WebRequest;
import org.springframework.web.servlet.mvc.method.annotation.ResponseEntityExceptionHandler;
import org.springframework.web.bind.annotation.ControllerAdvice;

@ControllerAdvice
public class ExceptionHandler extends ResponseEntityExceptionHandler {
```

```
    @Override
    protected ResponseEntity<Object> handleMethodArgumentNotValid(
        MethodArgumentNotValidException ex,
        HttpHeaders headers,
        HttpStatusCode status,
        WebRequest request) {

      return ResponseEntity.badRequest().body("Validation failed");
    }
}
```

LISTING 12-19: ExceptionHandler.java

Up to now, we have used simple validation, such as @NotNull, @NotBlank as well some regular expressions (for the credit card). If we need to have more complex validation, that checks more than one property at once, then we will have to introduce custom validation.

Although we have used validation in our frontend, it is always important to have the same (and even more) validations in the backend. This happens because client-side validations can be circumvented, allowing knowledgeable users to attack our backend and database.

In Spring Boot, a REST controller automatically performs validation on receipt of the HTTP request. Here, the OrderDTO validation is performed, as well as the validations of the contained objects, OrderDetailDTO and CreditCard.

We will first create a custom annotation:

```
package com.example.Eshop.validations;

import jakarta.validation.Constraint;
import jakarta.validation.Payload;
import java.lang.annotation.ElementType;
import java.lang.annotation.Retention;
import java.lang.annotation.RetentionPolicy;
import java.lang.annotation.Target;

@Constraint(validatedBy = ExpiredCardValidator.class)
@Target({ ElementType.TYPE })
@Retention(RetentionPolicy.RUNTIME)
public @interface NotExpired {
    String message() default "The card has expired";
    Class<?>[] groups() default {}; //groups parameter
    Class<? extends Payload>[] payload() default {}; //payload parameter
}
```

LISTING 12-20: NotExpired.java

Then, we will implement a custom validator:

package com.example.Eshop.validations;

```
import com.example.Eshop.dtos.CreditCardDTO;
import com.example.Eshop.dtos.OrderDTO;
import jakarta.validation.ConstraintValidator;
import jakarta.validation.ConstraintValidatorContext;

public class ExpiredCardValidator implements
    ConstraintValidator<NotExpired, OrderDTO> {

  @Override
  public boolean isValid(OrderDTO orderDTO, ConstraintValidatorContext context)
{
    if (orderDTO == null || orderDTO.getCreditCard() == null)
      return false;

    CreditCardDTO creditCard = orderDTO.getCreditCard();
    return !creditCard.isCardExpired();
  }
}
```

LISTING 12-21: ExpiredCardValidator.java

This custom validator will invoke the isCardExpired() method from the CreditCardDTO object and will return true or false.

For this to work, we have to add the custom annotation @NotExpired on the OrderDTO class:

@Data

@NotExpired //Use custom annotation

public class OrderDTO {

You may find the code for this chapter here:

https://github.com/htset/htset-eshop-angular-18-spring/tree/part12

13. Error handling and logging

In the previous chapter, we completed the product purchasing process, with the introduction of order validation and submission. One of the shortcomings of the web app, as it stands right now, is the lack of proper error handling and notification. If something goes wrong with the app (e.g. during order submission), the user will not be properly informed of the error. Moreover, the administrator of the app will also not be informed of any problems, as these errors will remain on the client side.

In this chapter, we will implement centralized error handling for our application. Moreover, we will introduce logging functionality on both front- and backend.

Error handling

We choose to implement a centralized solution for error handling, with the combined use of classes that extend the `ErrorHandler` and `HttpInterceptor` classes. The `GlobalErrorHandler` class handles general JavaScript errors and displays a modal dialog box containing the description of the error. It also reports the error to the backend, via the `RemoteLogging` service:

```
import { HttpErrorResponse } from "@angular/common/http";
import { ErrorHandler, Injectable } from "@angular/core";
import { LogMessage } from "../models/logMessage";
import { ErrorDialogService } from "../services/error-dialog.service";
import { LoggingService } from "../services/logging.service";

@Injectable()
export class GlobalErrorHandler implements ErrorHandler {

  constructor(private errorDialogService: ErrorDialogService,
    private remoteLoggingService: LoggingService) { }

  handleError(error: Error | HttpErrorResponse) {
    console.error("Error from global error handler", error);

    let errorMessage = "";
    let stackTrace = "";
    if (error instanceof HttpErrorResponse) {
      errorMessage = "An HTTP error occured. Status: " + error.status
    } else {
      errorMessage = "This operation resulted in an error";
      stackTrace = error.stack || '';
    }

    this.errorDialogService
      .openDialog(errorMessage);

    let logMessage: LogMessage
      = { message: errorMessage, stackTrace: stackTrace };
    this.remoteLoggingService.log(logMessage);
```

    }
}
```

LISTING 13-1: global-error-handler.ts

The `ErrorInterceptor` class intercepts HTTP requests and responses towards the backend and handles any errors pertaining to this interaction. The interceptor is also used to display a loading spinner during the communication with the backend:

```
import { Injectable } from '@angular/core';
import { HttpRequest, HttpHandler, HttpEvent, HttpInterceptor }
  from '@angular/common/http';
import { Observable, throwError } from 'rxjs';
import { catchError, finalize } from 'rxjs/operators';
import { LoadingDialogService } from '../services/loading-dialog.service';
import { AuthenticationService } from '../services/authentication.service';
import { StoreService } from '../services/store.service';

@Injectable()
export class ErrorInterceptor implements HttpInterceptor {

  constructor(private loadingDialogService: LoadingDialogService,
    private authenticationService: AuthenticationService,
    private storeService: StoreService) { }

  intercept(request: HttpRequest<any>, next: HttpHandler)
    : Observable<HttpEvent<any>> {
    const currentUser = this.storeService.user;
    this.loadingDialogService.openDialog();
    return next.handle(request).pipe(
      catchError(error => {
        console.error("Error from error interceptor", error);
        return throwError(() => error);
      }),
      finalize(() => {
        this.loadingDialogService.hideDialog();
      })
    ) as Observable<HttpEvent<any>>;
  }
}
```

LISTING 13-2: error-interceptor.ts

Both classes should be declared in app.module.ts, as `ErrorHandler` and `HTTP_INTERCEPTORS` respectively:

```
...
  providers: [
    provideAnimationsAsync(),
    {
      provide: HTTP_INTERCEPTORS,
```
```

```
      useClass: JwtInterceptor,
      multi: true
    },
    {
      provide: ErrorHandler,
      useClass: GlobalErrorHandler
    },
    {
      provide: HTTP_INTERCEPTORS,
      useClass: ErrorInterceptor,
      multi: true
    }
  ],
...
```

LISTING 13-3: app.module.ts

The `ErrorDialog` service uses the `NgbModal` service from Bootstrap for Angular to display a modal dialog box:

```
import { Injectable, Injector } from '@angular/core';
import { NgbModal, NgbModalRef } from '@ng-bootstrap/ng-bootstrap';
import { ErrorDialogComponent } from '../components/shared/error-dialog/error-dialog.component';

@Injectable({
  providedIn: 'root'
})
export class ErrorDialogService {

  private opened = false;
  private dialogRef?: NgbModalRef;
  private modalService?: NgbModal;

  constructor(private injector: Injector) { }

  openDialog(message: string, info?: string): void {
    if (!this.opened) {
      this.opened = true;
      this.modalService = this.injector.get(NgbModal);
      this.dialogRef = this.modalService.open(ErrorDialogComponent);
      this.dialogRef.componentInstance.message.set(message);
      this.dialogRef.componentInstance.info.set(info);

      this.dialogRef?.closed.subscribe(() => {
        this.opened = false;
      });
    }
  }

  hideDialog() {
    this.dialogRef?.close();
  }
```

}

LISTING 13-4: error-dialog.service.ts

We use the Injector object to manually inject the NgbModal service, because when we try to inject it in the component's constructor, we get a Circular Dependency error.

This dialog box is defined as a component (ErrorDialogComponent) that contains two strings:

```html
<div class="modal-header">
  <h4 class="modal-title" id="modal-basic-title">Error</h4>
</div>
<div class="modal-body">
  <p class="error-message">
    {{message()}}
  </p>
  @if(info()){
  <p>
    <em>Additional information: {{info()}}</em>
  </p>
  }
</div>
<div class="modal-footer">
  <button type="button" class="btn btn-outline-dark"
          (click)="activeModal.close()">
    Close
  </button>
</div>
```

LISTING 13-5: error-dialog.component.html

We get access to those strings from the outside of the class, with the use of signals:

```typescript
import { Component, OnInit, input, signal } from '@angular/core';
import { NgbActiveModal } from '@ng-bootstrap/ng-bootstrap';

@Component({
  selector: 'app-error-dialog',
  templateUrl: './error-dialog.component.html',
  styleUrls: ['./error-dialog.component.css']
})
export class ErrorDialogComponent implements OnInit {

  message = signal("");
  info = signal("");

  constructor(public activeModal: NgbActiveModal) { }

  ngOnInit(): void {
  }
}
```

LISTING 13-6: error-dialog.component.ts

Note: Now that we have the global error handling in place, it is a good idea to remove the localized error handling in the services. For example, we can change the ItemService like this:

...

```
  getItems(page: number, pageSize: number, filter: Filter)
    : Observable<ItemPayload> {
    let categoriesString: string = "";
    filter.categories
      .forEach(cc => categoriesString = categoriesString + cc + "#");
    if (categoriesString.length > 0)
      categoriesString = categoriesString
        .substring(0, categoriesString.length - 1);

    let params = new HttpParams()
      .set("name", filter.name)
      .set("pageNumber", page.toString())
      .set("pageSize", pageSize.toString())
      .set("category", categoriesString);

    return this.http.get<ItemPayload>(this.itemsUrl, { params: params })
      .pipe(
        catchError(this.handleError<ItemPayload>('getItems',
          { items: [], count: 0 }))
      );
  }

  getItem(id: number): Observable<Item> {
    const url = `${this.itemsUrl}/${id}`;
    return this.http.get<Item>(url)
      .pipe(
        catchError(this.handleError<Item>(`getItem/${id}`,
          { id: 0, name: "", price: 0, category: "", description: "" }))
      );
  }
```

...

LISTING 13-7: item.service.ts

In other places, we have chosen to keep error handling locally, e.g. in the Login component:

...

```
  onSubmit() {
    this.submitted = true;

    if (this.loginForm.invalid)
```

```
        return;
      this.loading = true;
      this.authenticationService.login(
        this.loginForm.controls['username'].value,
        this.loginForm.controls['password'].value
      )
        .subscribe({
          next: () => {
            const returnUrl
              = this.route.snapshot.queryParams['returnUrl'] || '/';
            this.router.navigate([returnUrl]);
          },
          error: error => {
            this.error = error.error.message;
            this.loading = false;
          }
        });
  }
...
```

LISTING 13-8: login.component.ts

This will override global error handling, as the login component will eventually handle the error.

Loading spinner

We create a loading spinner that will appear to the users as a pop-up dialog. The new component has the following template:

```
<div class="d-flex justify-content-center">
  <div class="spinner-border" role="status"></div>
</div>
```

LISTING 13-9: loading-dialog.component.html

We also have to create a new service (LoadingDialogService) that will handle the opening of the dialog:

```
import { Injectable } from '@angular/core';
import { NgbModal, NgbModalRef } from '@ng-bootstrap/ng-bootstrap';
import { LoadingDialogComponent }
  from '../components/shared/loading-dialog/loading-dialog.component';

@Injectable({
  providedIn: 'root'
})
export class LoadingDialogService {
  private opened = false;
```

```typescript
  private dialogRef?: NgbModalRef;

  constructor(private modalService: NgbModal) { }

  openDialog(): void {
    if (!this.opened) {
      this.opened = true;
      this.dialogRef = this.modalService.open(LoadingDialogComponent);

      this.dialogRef?.closed.subscribe(() => {
        this.opened = false;
      });
    }
  }
  hideDialog() {
    this.dialogRef?.close();
  }
}
```

LISTING 13-10: loading-dialog.service.ts

Logging

One of the most important features of web application functionality is logging. With logging, we can be informed of how the application is used and of any errors that may happen.

Spring Boot, for example, comes with a built-in support for SLF4J (Simple Logging Facade for Java) and Logback, but we can also use Log4j2 or other logging frameworks.

We start with adding the required dependencies:

```xml
<dependency>
    <groupId>org.springframework.boot</groupId>
    <artifactId>spring-boot-starter-log4j2</artifactId>
</dependency>
```

LISTING 13-11: pom.xml

Then, we add logging configuration info into *application.properties* file:

```
...

logging.level.org.springframework=INFO
logging.level.com.example.Eshop=INFO
logging.file.name=app.log
logging.pattern.console=%d{yyyy-MM-dd HH:mm:ss} - %msg%n
```

LISTING 13-12: application.properties

Here we define the file that the logs will be stored into (*app.log*) and the selected log level (INFO).

Now that we have set up the logging mechanism, we can use it in our project. Remember, errors that happen in the Angular app will be displayed only to the end-user, as we have yet no mechanism to inform ourselves of any problems in the app. For this reason, we create a new controller (RemoteLoggingController) that will receive error messages from the frontend and will store them in the Logs table:

```java
package com.example.Eshop.controllers;

import com.example.Eshop.dtos.LogMessageDTO;
import org.slf4j.Logger;
import org.slf4j.LoggerFactory;
import org.springframework.http.ResponseEntity;
import org.springframework.web.bind.annotation.PostMapping;
import org.springframework.web.bind.annotation.RequestBody;
import org.springframework.web.bind.annotation.RequestMapping;
import org.springframework.web.bind.annotation.RestController;

@RestController
@RequestMapping("/remoteLogging")
public class RemoteLoggingController {
  private final Logger logger
    = LoggerFactory.getLogger(RemoteLoggingController.class);
  @PostMapping
  public ResponseEntity<?> postLog(@RequestBody LogMessageDTO logMessage) {
    switch(logMessage.getLevel()){
      case "Info":
        logger.info(logMessage.getMessage());
        break;
      case "Warn":
        logger.warn(logMessage.getMessage());
        break;
      case "Error":
        logger.error(logMessage.getMessage()
            + " - Stack trace: " + logMessage.getStackTrace());
        break;
      default:
        logger.info(logMessage.getMessage());
        break;
    }

    return ResponseEntity.ok().build();
  }
}
```

LISTING 13-13: RemoteLoggingController.java

We should also define the LogMessageDTO class:

```java
package com.example.Eshop.dtos;
```

```java
import lombok.Data;
@Data
public class LogMessageDTO {
  private String message;
  private String level;
  private String stackTrace;
}
```

LISTING 13-14: LogMessageDTO.java

Moreover, we should modify the SecurityConfig class, so that it allows logging messages without authentication, since the users may not have logged during browsing the items catalog:

```java
...
    @Bean
    public SecurityFilterChain securityFilterChain(HttpSecurity http)
        throws Exception {
      http
          //Disable CSRF since this is a stateless REST API
          .csrf(csrf -> csrf.disable())
          //Enable CORS
          .cors(cors -> cors.configurationSource(corsConfigurationSource()))
          //Define public endpoints that can be accessed without authentication
          .authorizeHttpRequests(auth -> auth
                  .requestMatchers("/users/**").hasRole("ADMIN")
                  .requestMatchers(
                      "/auth/**",
                      "/items/**",
                      "/remoteLogging/**").permitAll()   // Allow access to auth endpoints
                  .anyRequest().authenticated()   // All other endpoints get authentication
          )
          //Add JWT token filter before UsernamePasswordAuthenticationFilter
                  .addFilterBefore(jwtRequestFilter,
              UsernamePasswordAuthenticationFilter.class);

      return http.build();
    }
...
```

LISTING 13-15: SecurityConfig.java

In the frontend, we create a new Angular service (LoggingService) that posts client-side errors to the backend. As we saw earlier, this service is used in the global error handler:

```
import { HttpClient, HttpHeaders } from '@angular/common/http';
import { Injectable } from '@angular/core';
```

```
import { environment } from '../../environments/environment';
import { LogMessage } from '../models/logMessage';

@Injectable({
  providedIn: 'root'
})
export class LoggingService {

  httpOptions = {
    headers: new HttpHeaders({ 'Content-Type': 'application/json' })
  };

  constructor(private http: HttpClient) { }

  log(logMessage: LogMessage) {
    this.http.post<LogMessage>(`${environment.apiUrl}/remoteLogging`,
logMessage)
      .subscribe();
  }
}
```

LISTING 13-16: logging.service.ts

We also add the `LogMessage` structure:

```
export interface LogMessage {
  message: string,
  level: string,
  stackTrace: string
}
```

LISTING 13-17: logMessage.ts

Bonus stuff: Analytics

Analytics is another valuable source of information for the developers of a web application. With analytics, we can understand how the end-users make use of the application (i.e., which pages they usually visit and which buttons they press).

There are specialized platforms for those operations that can provide us with valuable insights into app usage. We will just use this opportunity to show how we can use *Directives* to implement cross-cutting features in our code.

We create a new Directive, called `AnalyticsDirective`, inside a new folder (/src/app/directives):

```
import { Directive, ElementRef, HostListener, Input } from '@angular/core';
import { Router } from '@angular/router';
```

```typescript
@Directive({
  selector: '[appAnalytics]'
})
export class AnalyticsDirective {

  @Input("events") events: string = "";

  constructor(private el: ElementRef,
    private router: Router) { }

  @HostListener('click') onClick() {
    if (this.events.indexOf('click') >= 0) {
      this.logEvent("click");
    }
  }

  @HostListener('change') onInput() {
    if (this.events.indexOf('change') >= 0) {
      this.logEvent("change");
    }
  }

  @HostListener('blur') onBlur() {
    if (this.events.indexOf('blur') >= 0) {
      this.logEvent("blur");
    }
  }

  logEvent(eventName: string) {
    console.log("Event: " + eventName);
    console.log("Element ID: " + this.el.nativeElement.id);
    console.log("Element value: " + this.el.nativeElement.value)
    console.log("Page: " + this.router.url)
  }
}
```

LISTING 13-18: analytics.directive.ts

For the directive to work, we have to apply it to one or more components, by adding the addAnalytics selector:

```
@for(item of storeService.cart.cartItems; track item){
<tr>

...
  <td>
    <input type="number" [(ngModel)]="item.quantity"
      size="2" id="quantity"
      appAnalytics events="change blur" />
  </td>
...
  <td>
    <input type="button" (click)="removeFromCart(item)"
```

```
        id="remove" value="Remove"
        appAnalytics events="click" />
    </td>
...
<button (click)="emptyCart()" id="empty"
  [disabled]="storeService.cart.cartItems.length == 0"
  appAnalytics events="click">Empty Cart
</button>
</tr>
```

LISTING 13-19: cart.component.html

Here, we apply the directive to the *Remove from Cart* button and the *Quantity* input box on the *Show Cart* page. Next to the `appAnalytics` selector, we add the `events` attribute. This attribute defines the DOM events that the directive should listen to and send to the analytics provider.

The `@HostListener` attribute is the way for the Directive to listen to the HTML element's events. Also, the `ElementRef` object can be used to gain access to the element's attibutes, like id and value.

In this simple example, the directive just displays the analytics information on the console log, instead of a specialized platform.

You may find the code for this chapter here:

https://github.com/htset/htset-eshop-angular-18-spring/tree/part13

14. User registration

In this chapter, we will delve into the details of user registration. We will also see how to help users reset their passwords, when they forget them.

Registration request

First of all, let's create the registration form component:

```
<h2>Registration</h2>
<div class="card">
  <div class="card-body" id="cartBody">
    <form [formGroup]="registrationForm" (ngSubmit)="onSubmit()">
      <div class="form-row">
        <div class="form-group col-md-2">
          <label for="firstName">First Name:</label>
          <input type="text" formControlName="firstName"
                 class="form-control form-control-sm"
                 [ngClass]="{   'is-invalid':   submitted()   ==   true   &&
registrationForm.controls['firstName'].errors }" />
          @if(registrationForm.controls['firstName'].invalid
          && (registrationForm.controls['firstName'].dirty
          || registrationForm.controls['firstName'].touched)){
          <div class="text-danger">
            @if(registrationForm.controls['firstName']
               && registrationForm.controls['firstName'].errors?.['required']){
            <div>
              First name is required
            </div>
            }
            @if(registrationForm.controls['firstName'].errors?.['minlength']){
            <div>
              First name must be at least 1 character long
            </div>
            }
          </div>
          }
        </div>
      </div>
      <div class="form-row">
        <div class="form-group col-md-2">
          <label for="lastName">Last Name:</label>
          <input   type="text"   formControlName="lastName"   class="form-control form-control-sm"
                 [ngClass]="{   'is-invalid':   submitted()   ==   true   &&
registrationForm.controls['lastName'].errors }" />
          @if(registrationForm.controls['lastName'].invalid
          && (registrationForm.controls['lastName'].dirty
          || registrationForm.controls['lastName'].touched)){
          <div class="text-danger">
            @if(registrationForm.controls['lastName'].errors?.['required']){
            <div>
              Last name is required
```

```html
          </div>
        }
        @if(registrationForm.controls['lastName'].errors?.['minlength']){
          <div>
            Last name must be at least 1 character long
          </div>
        }
      </div>
      }
    </div>
  </div>
  <div class="form-row">
    <div class="form-group col-md-2">
      <label for="username">User Name:</label>
      <input    type="text"    formControlName="username"    class="form-control form-control-sm"
            [ngClass]="{   'is-invalid':   submitted()   ==   true   && registrationForm.controls['username'].errors }" />
      @if(registrationForm.controls['username'].invalid
        && (registrationForm.controls['username'].dirty
          || registrationForm.controls['username'].touched)){
        <div class="text-danger">
          @if(registrationForm.controls['username'].errors?.['required']){
          <div>
            Username is required
          </div>
          }
          @if(registrationForm.controls['username'].errors?.['minlength']){
          <div>
            Username must be at least 4 characters long
          </div>
          }
        </div>
      }
    </div>
  </div>
  <div class="form-row">
    <div class="form-group col-md-2">
      <label for="password">Password:</label>
      <input   type="password"   formControlName="password"   class="form-control form-control-sm"
            [ngClass]="{   'is-invalid':   submitted()   ==   true   && registrationForm.controls['password'].errors }" />
      @if(registrationForm.controls['password'].invalid
        && (registrationForm.controls['password'].dirty
          || registrationForm.controls['password'].touched)){
      <div class="text-danger">
        @if(registrationForm.controls['password'].errors?.['required']){
        <div>
          Password is required
        </div>
        }
      </div>
      }
    </div>
```

```
      </div>
    <div class="form-row">
      <div class="form-group col-md-2">
        <label for="confirmPassword">Confirm password:</label>
        <input type="password" formControlName="confirmPassword" class="form-control form-control-sm"
            [ngClass]="{ 'is-invalid': submitted() == true && registrationForm.controls['confirmPassword'].errors && registrationForm.errors?.['passwordsMustMatch'] }" />
        @if((registrationForm.controls['confirmPassword'].invalid
          || registrationForm.errors?.['passwordsMustMatch'])
         && (registrationForm.controls['confirmPassword'].dirty
          || registrationForm.controls['confirmPassword'].touched)){
        <div class="text-danger">
          @if(registrationForm.controls['confirmPassword'].errors?.['required']){
          <div>
            Confirm Password is required
          </div>
          }
          @if(registrationForm.errors?.['passwordsMustMatch']){
          <div>
            Passwords must match
          </div>
          }
        </div>
        }
      </div>
    </div>
    <div class="form-row">
      <div class="form-group col-md-2">
        <label for="email">Email:</label>
        <input type="text" formControlName="email" class="form-control form-control-sm"
            [ngClass]="{ 'is-invalid': submitted() == true && registrationForm.controls['email'].errors }" />
        @if(registrationForm.controls['email'].invalid
          && (registrationForm.controls['email'].dirty
           || registrationForm.controls['email'].touched)){
        <div class="text-danger">
          @if(registrationForm.controls['email'].errors?.['required']){
          <div>
            Email is required
          </div>
          }
          @if(registrationForm.controls['email'].errors?.['email']){
          <div>
            Email must be a valid email address
          </div>
          }
        </div>
        }
      </div>
    </div>
    <re-captcha formControlName="recaptcha"
```

```html
                     (resolved)="onCaptchaResolved($event)"
                     siteKey="6LfxP8IfAAAAACCm4xcrhmBi5jL9vKnG4tfoCu2D"></re-
captcha>
      <button type="submit"
              [disabled]="!registrationForm.valid">
        Register
      </button>
    </form>
  </div>

  @if(success() && submitted()){
  <div class="alert alert-success" role="alert">
    Registration was successful. A confirmation email has been sent to:
    {{this.registrationForm.controls.email.value}} <br />
    <button routerLink="/{{this.returnUrl()}}">Continue</button>
  </div>
  }

  @if(!success() && submitted()){
  <div class="alert alert-danger" role="alert">{{errorMessage()}}</div>
  }
</div>
```

LISTING 14-1: registration.component.html

```typescript
import { Component, OnInit, signal } from '@angular/core';
import { FormControl, FormGroup, Validators } from '@angular/forms';
import { ActivatedRoute, Router } from '@angular/router';
import { UserService } from '../../../../app/services/user.service';
import { passwordsMustMatchValidator }
  from '../../../../app/validators/passwordsMustMatch';

@Component({
  selector: 'app-registration',
  templateUrl: './registration.component.html',
  styleUrls: ['./registration.component.css']
})
export class RegistrationComponent implements OnInit {
  submitted = signal<boolean>(false);
  success =signal<boolean>(false);
  errorMessage = signal<string>("");
  returnUrl = signal<string>('/');
  captchaResolved = signal<boolean>(false);

  registrationForm = new FormGroup({
    firstName: new FormControl('',
      [Validators.required, Validators.minLength(1)]),
    lastName: new FormControl('',
      [Validators.required, Validators.minLength(1)]),
    username: new FormControl('',
      [Validators.required, Validators.minLength(4)]),
    password: new FormControl('',
      Validators.required),
```

```typescript
    confirmPassword: new FormControl('',
      Validators.required),
    email: new FormControl('',
      [Validators.required, Validators.email]),
    recaptcha: new FormControl('',
      [Validators.required])
  }, { validators: [passwordsMustMatchValidator] });

  constructor(private userService: UserService,
    public route: ActivatedRoute) { }

  ngOnInit(): void {
  }

  onSubmit() {
    console.warn(this.registrationForm.value);
    this.submitted.set(true);
    if (!this.registrationForm.valid)
      return;

    this.userService.addUser({
      firstName: this.registrationForm.controls['firstName'].value || '',
      lastName: this.registrationForm.controls['lastName'].value || '',
      username: this.registrationForm.controls['username'].value || '',
      password: this.registrationForm.controls['password'].value || '',
      email: this.registrationForm.controls['email'].value || ''
    })
      .subscribe({
        next: () => {
          this.success.set(true);
          this.registrationForm.disable();
          this.returnUrl.set(this.route.snapshot.queryParams['returnUrl']
            || '/');
        },
        error: error => {
          this.success.set(false);
          this.errorMessage = error.error;
        }
      });
  }

  onCaptchaResolved(result: string | null) {
    this.captchaResolved.set((result) ? true : false);
  }
}
```

LISTING 14-2: registration.component.ts

The registration component consists of a reactive form, in the same way as we have seen in previous chapters. However, there is some new stuff that we should talk about.

In addition to per-control validation, this form includes also validation on two controls combined (*password* and *confirmPassword* text boxes). To implement this, we create a validator function in a new folder called `validators`:

```
import {
  AbstractControl, FormGroup,
  ValidationErrors, ValidatorFn
} from "@angular/forms";

export const passwordsMustMatchValidator: ValidatorFn =
  (control: AbstractControl): ValidationErrors | null => {
    const p = control.get('password');
    const rp = control.get('confirmPassword');

    if (rp?.errors) {
      //return if another validator has already
      //found an error on the matchingControl
      return null;
    }
    return p && rp && p.value !== rp.value ?
      { passwordsMustMatch: true } : null;
  }
```

LISTING 14-3: passwordsMustMatch.ts

This validator is used on the `registrationForm` form group as a whole and not on a specific form control. It accesses the contents of both controls and checks if they are equal.

Furthermore, notice that we handle any errors that happen during registration locally, and not through the centralized error control that we introduced in the previous chapter. When we subscribe to the Observable returned from `addUser()` function in `UserService`, we also pass an error handling function that will display the error message on the page and not in a message box. If we omit this function, then the centralized error handling will kick in and will display a message box with the error message.

By the way, function `addUser()` should be defined in `UserService`:

```
...
  addUser(user: User) {
    return this.http
      .post<User>(`${environment.apiUrl}/auth/register`, user,
          this.httpOptions);
  }
...
```

LISTING 14-4: user.service.ts

Finally, apart from the usual text controls, the form contains a Recaptcha control, to verify that the requester is not a bot. In order to use the Recaptcha control we have to create a Recaptcha account with Google at https://www.google.com/recaptcha/.

We choose to register a new v2 Racaptcha site and we get a site key that we include in the Recaptcha component (`<re-captcha>`) in the html template. We also implement the `onCaptchaResolved()` callback function that is called upon user verification.

The Recaptcha component is installed with the following:

```
npm install ng-recaptcha-2
```

We will also have to include the `RecaptchaFormsModule` and `RecaptchaModule` modules in app.module.ts file:

```
import { RecaptchaFormsModule, RecaptchaModule } from 'ng-recaptcha-2';
...
  imports: [
    ...
    RecaptchaModule,
    RecaptchaFormsModule
  ],
...
```

LISTING 15-5: app.module.ts

We will also have to add the `/register` route in app-routing.module.ts file.

On the backend side now, we create the Register function that handles calls to `/auth/register`:

```
...

  private MailConfig mailConfig;

  public AuthController(AuthenticationManager authenticationManager,
                        CustomUserDetailsService userDetailsService,
                        UserService userService, JwtUtilities jwtUtilities,
                        PasswordEncoder passwordEncoder,
                        MailConfig mailConfig){
    this.authenticationManager = authenticationManager;
    this.userDetailsService = userDetailsService;
    this.userService = userService;
    this.jwtUtilities = jwtUtilities;
    this.passwordEncoder = passwordEncoder;
    this.mailConfig = mailConfig;
  }

  //Register new user
  @PostMapping("/register")
  public ResponseEntity<?> registerUser(@RequestBody User user) {
```

```java
        try {
          //Check if the username or email already exists
          if (userService.getUserByUsername(user.getUsername()) != null) {
            return ResponseEntity.badRequest().body("Username already exists");
          }
          if (userService.getUserByEmail(user.getEmail()) != null) {
            return ResponseEntity.badRequest().body("Email already exists");
          }

          //Hash the password before saving
          user.setPassword(passwordEncoder.encode(user.getPassword()));
          user.setRole("CUSTOMER");
          user.setStatus("PENDING");
          user.setRegistrationCode(createConfirmationToken());

          User createdUser = userService.updateUser(user);

          sendConfirmationEmail(createdUser);

          return ResponseEntity.ok(createDTO(createdUser));
        } catch (Exception e) {
          return ResponseEntity.status(HttpStatus.INTERNAL_SERVER_ERROR)
              .body("Registration failed: " + e.getMessage());
        }
      }

...

    public String createConfirmationToken() {
      byte[] randomNum = new byte[64];
      SecureRandom secureRandom = new SecureRandom();
      //Fill array with secure random bytes
      secureRandom.nextBytes(randomNum);
      //Encode bytes to Base64
      String tempString = Base64.getEncoder().encodeToString(randomNum);
      //Replace problematic characters
      return tempString
          .replace("+", "")
          .replace("=", "")
          .replace("/", "");
    }

...

private void sendConfirmationEmail(User user) {
    //Get mail server properties
    Properties props = new Properties();
    props.put("mail.smtp.host", mailConfig.getSmtpHost());
    props.put("mail.smtp.port", mailConfig.getSmtpPort());
    props.put("mail.smtp.auth", String.valueOf(mailConfig.isSmtpAuth()));
    props.put("mail.smtp.starttls.enable",
        String.valueOf(mailConfig.isStarttlsEnable()));
    props.put("mail.smtp.ssl.trust", mailConfig.getSslTrust());

    //Create a session with an authenticator
```

```java
    Session session = Session.getInstance(props, new Authenticator() {
      @Override
      protected PasswordAuthentication getPasswordAuthentication() {
        return new PasswordAuthentication(mailConfig.getSmtpUsername(),
            mailConfig.getSmtpPassword());
      }
    });

    try {
      //Create Message
      Message message = new MimeMessage(session);
      message.setFrom(new InternetAddress("info@my-eshop.com"));
      message.setSubject("Confirm Registration");
      message.setContent(
          "To confirm registration please click "
              +" <a href=\"http://localhost:4200/confirm_registration?code="
              + user.getRegistrationCode()
              + "\">here</a>",
          "text/html" //Body is HTML
      );
      message.setRecipient(Message.RecipientType.TO,
          new InternetAddress(user.getEmail()));

      //Send message
      Transport.send(message);
    } catch (MessagingException e) {
      e.printStackTrace();
    }
  }

...
```

LISTING 14-6: AuthController.java

We also add the following methods in *UserService.java*:

...

```java
  public User getUserByUsername(String username) {
    return userRepository.findByUsername(username);
  }

  public User getUserByEmail(String email) {
    return userRepository.findByEmail(email);
  }
```

...

LISTING 14-7: UserService.java

After we check that the supplied username and the email do not already exist, we create a new user with *Pending* status and we send him an email with a confirmation code.

This code is a randomly generated base64 string, where we replace the \, /, + and = characters that don't play well in URLs. We see that the email body contains a link to the registration confirmation page, in the form of:

```
https://localhost:4200/confirm_registration?code=xxxxxxxx
```

where xxxxxxxx is the registration code.

The SMTP server settings have been added to the *application.properties* file:

```
...

mail.smtp.host=smtp.example.com
mail.smtp.port=587
mail.smtp.username=your_email@example.com
mail.smtp.password=your_password
mail.smtp.auth=true
mail.smtp.starttls.enable=true
mail.smtp.ssl.trust=smtp.example.com
```

LISTING 14-8: application.properties

To read those application properties in the controller, we create a new class (`MailConfig`) in the `config` package:

```
package com.example.Eshop.config;

import lombok.Data;
import org.springframework.beans.factory.annotation.Value;
import org.springframework.stereotype.Component;

@Data
@Component
public class MailConfig {
  @Value("${mail.smtp.host}")
  private String smtpHost;

  @Value("${mail.smtp.port}")
  private int smtpPort;

  @Value("${mail.smtp.username}")
  private String smtpUsername;

  @Value("${mail.smtp.password}")
  private String smtpPassword;

  @Value("${mail.smtp.auth}")
  private boolean smtpAuth;
```

```java
    @Value("${mail.smtp.starttls.enable}")
    private boolean starttlsEnable;

    @Value("${mail.smtp.ssl.trust}")
    private String sslTrust;
}
```

LISTING 14-9: MailConfig.java

Next, we have to add the `RegistrationCode` fields into the `User` model:

```java
package com.example.Eshop.models;

import jakarta.persistence.*;
import lombok.*;

import java.util.Date;

@Data
@NoArgsConstructor
@AllArgsConstructor
@Entity
public class User {
  @Id
  @GeneratedValue(strategy = GenerationType.IDENTITY)
  private Long id;
  private String username;
  private String password;
  private String firstName;
  private String lastName;
  private String email;
  private String status;
  private String role;
  private String token;
  private String refreshToken;
  private Date refreshTokenExpiry;
  private String registrationCode;
}
```

LISTING 14-10: User.java

Moreover, we add a new method in UserRepository:

```java
package com.example.Eshop.repositories;

import com.example.Eshop.models.User;
import org.springframework.data.jpa.repository.JpaRepository;

public interface UserRepository extends JpaRepository<User, Long> {
  User findByUsername(String username);
  User findByEmail(String email);
```

}

LISTING 14-11: UserRepository.java

Finally, we have to add the necessary dependencies for sending mail:

```xml
<dependency>
  <groupId>javax.mail</groupId>
  <artifactId>javax.mail-api</artifactId>
  <version>1.6.2</version>
</dependency>
<dependency>
  <groupId>com.sun.mail</groupId>
    <artifactId>javax.mail</artifactId>
    <version>1.6.2</version>
  </dependency>
```

LISTING 14-12: pom.xml

Registration confirmation

Next, we create the registration confirmation component. This is where the user will land when he follows the link in the email:

```html
<h3>Registration E-mail Confirmation</h3>
<p>{{result}}</p>
<p><button routerLink="/">Go to product list</button></p>
@if(storeService.cart.cartItems.length > 0
  && storeService.cart.isCartValid()){
<p>
  <button routerLink="/cart">Go to cart</button>
</p>
}
```

LISTING 14-13: registration-confirm.component.html

```typescript
import { Component, OnInit } from '@angular/core';
import { ActivatedRoute, Router } from '@angular/router';
import { map, mergeMap, tap } from 'rxjs/operators';
import { StoreService } from '../../../../app/services/store.service';
import { UserService } from '../../../../app/services/user.service';

@Component({
  selector: 'app-registration-confirm',
  templateUrl: './registration-confirm.component.html',
  styleUrls: ['./registration-confirm.component.css']
})
export class RegistrationConfirmComponent implements OnInit {
```

```typescript
  result: string = "";

  constructor(
    private route: ActivatedRoute,
    private userService: UserService,
    public storeService: StoreService,
    private router: Router
  ) { }

  ngOnInit(): void {
    let code = '';
    this.route.queryParams.pipe(
      tap(params => code = params['code']),
      mergeMap(params => this.userService.confirmRegistration(code)),
      map(user => {
        sessionStorage.setItem('user', JSON.stringify(user));
        this.storeService.user = user;
        return user;
      })
    )
      .subscribe({
        next: () => {
          this.result = "Registration was successfully confirmed";
        },
        error: error => {
          this.result = "Registration confirmation failed. " + error.error;
        }
      });
  }
}
```

LISTING 14-14: registration-confirm.component.ts

When the component is loaded, it retrieves the registration code from the query string and calls the `confirmRegistration` function in `UserService`. After the registration has been confirmed, the user is automatically logged in (we set the user object in the session storage).

Note here the use of `mergeMap()` function of RxJS. The process of retrieving the query string is asynchronous. To achieve calling `confirmRegistration()` in sequence, i.e. only after the confirmation code has been retrieved from the query string, we use `pipe()` and `mergeMap()`.

We should also add `confirmRegistration` function in `UserService`:

```typescript
...
  confirmRegistration(code: string) {
    return this.http
      .post<User>(`${environment.apiUrl}/auth/confirm_registration`,
        { code: code }, this.httpOptions);
  }
...
```

LISTING 14-15: user.service.ts

Also, remember to add the /confirm_registration route to *app-routing.module.ts* file.

On the API side, here is the respective method called:

...

```java
  @PostMapping("/confirm_registration")
  public ResponseEntity<?> confirmRegistration(@RequestBody RegistrationCodeDTO code) {
    try{
      // Retrieve user by registration code
      User user = userService.getUserByRegistrationCode(code.getCode());

      if (user == null) {
        return ResponseEntity.badRequest().body("Registration code not found");
      }

      // Check if the user is already activated
      if ("ACTIVE".equals(user.getStatus())) {
        return ResponseEntity.badRequest().body("User is already activated");
      }

      // Activate user and generate tokens
      user.setStatus("ACTIVE");
      String token = jwtUtilities
          .generateToken(user.getUsername(), user.getId(), user.getRole());
      String refreshToken = jwtUtilities
          .generateRefreshToken(user.getUsername());
      user.setToken(token);
      user.setRefreshToken(refreshToken);
      user.setRefreshTokenExpiry(new Date(System.currentTimeMillis()
          + 1000 * 60 * 60 * 24 * 30));   //30 days expiry

      userService.updateUser(user);    //Save user changes

      return ResponseEntity.ok(createDTO(user));
    } catch (Exception e) {
      return ResponseEntity.status(HttpStatus.INTERNAL_SERVER_ERROR)
          .body("Failed to confirm registration: " + e.getMessage());
    }
  }
```

...

LISTING 14-16: AuthController.java

Note here that we define a special purpose class (`RegistrationCodeDTO`) that will be used by Spring to bind and validate the HTTP request payload body and to make it available for us in the method body. Here is its definition:

```java
package com.example.Eshop.dtos;

import lombok.Data;

@Data
public class RegistrationCodeDTO {
  private String code;
}
```

LISTING 14-17 RegistrationCodeDTO.java

We need to add a new method in UserService:

```java
...

  public User getUserByRegistrationCode(String registrationCode) {
    return userRepository.findByRegistrationCode(registrationCode);
  }

...
```

LISTING 14-18 UserService.java

Also, we add the respective method in UserRepository:

```java
package com.example.Eshop.repositories;

import com.example.Eshop.models.User;
import org.springframework.data.jpa.repository.JpaRepository;

public interface UserRepository extends JpaRepository<User, Long> {
  User findByUsername(String username);
  User findByEmail(String email);
  User findByRegistrationCode(String registrationCode);
}
```

LISTING 14-19 UserRepository.java

Finally, we have to update our Controller so that users may login only when they are in the *Active* state:

```java
...

  @PostMapping("/login")
  public ResponseEntity<?> login(@RequestBody AuthRequestDTO authRequest)
      throws Exception {
```

```java
    //Use username and password to authenticate user
    try {
      authenticationManager.authenticate(
          new UsernamePasswordAuthenticationToken(authRequest.getUsername(),
              authRequest.getPassword())
      );

      CustomUserDetails userDetails =
          (CustomUserDetails)userDetailsService
              .loadUserByUsername(authRequest.getUsername());

      if(!userDetails.isEnabled()){
        return ResponseEntity.status(HttpStatus.BAD_REQUEST)
            .body("Registration has not been confirmed");
      }

      //Generate JWT tokens
      String token = jwtUtilities.generateToken(userDetails.getUsername(),
          userDetails.getId(), userDetails.getRole());
      String refreshToken = jwtUtilities
          .generateRefreshToken(userDetails.getUsername());

      //Save token to database
      User user = userService.getUserById(userDetails.getId());
      user.setToken(token);
      user.setRefreshToken(refreshToken);
      user.setRefreshTokenExpiry(new Date(System.currentTimeMillis()
          + 1000L * 60 * 60 * 24 * 30)); // 30-day expiry
      userService.updateUser(user);

      return ResponseEntity.ok(this.createDTO(user));
    } catch (BadCredentialsException e) {
      return ResponseEntity.status(HttpStatus.UNAUTHORIZED)
          .body("Invalid credentials");
    } catch (UsernameNotFoundException e) {
      return ResponseEntity.status(HttpStatus.UNAUTHORIZED)
          .body("Invalid credentials");
    } catch (Exception e) {
      return ResponseEntity.status(HttpStatus.INTERNAL_SERVER_ERROR)
          .body("Authentication failed: " + e.getMessage());
    }
  }
}

...
```

LISTING 14-20 UserController.cs

Forgot password

This is the component used for the password reset request:

```
<h2>Password Reset</h2>
<div class="card">
```

```
<div class="card-body" id="cartBody">
  <form [formGroup]="forgotForm" (ngSubmit)="onSubmit()">
    <div class="form-row">
      <div class="form-group col-md-2">
        <label for="email">
          Please type your email address:
        </label>
        <input type="text"
               formControlName="email"
               class="form-control form-control-sm"
               [ngClass]="{ 'is-invalid': submitted() == true && forgotForm.controls['email'].errors }" />
        @if(forgotForm.controls['email'].invalid
        && (forgotForm.controls['email'].dirty
        || forgotForm.controls['email'].touched)){
        <div class="text-danger">
          @if(forgotForm.controls['email'].errors?.['required']){
          <div>
            Email is required
          </div>
          }
          @if(forgotForm.controls['email'].errors?.['email']){
          <div>
            Email must be a valid email address
          </div>
          }
        </div>
        }
      </div>
    </div>
    <button type="submit"
            [disabled]="!forgotForm.valid">
      Submit
    </button>
  </form>
</div>
@if(success() && submitted()){
<div class="alert alert-success" role="alert">
  Password was reset successful.
  An email with instructions has been sent to:
  {{this.forgotForm.controls['email'].value}}
</div>
}

@if(!success() && submitted()){
<div class="alert alert-danger" role="alert">
  {{errorMessage()}}
</div>
}
</div>
```

LISTING 14-21: forgot-password.component.html

```typescript
import { Component, OnInit, signal } from '@angular/core';
import { FormControl, FormGroup, Validators } from '@angular/forms';
import { UserService } from '../../../../app/services/user.service';

@Component({
  selector: 'app-forgot-password',
  templateUrl: './forgot-password.component.html',
  styleUrls: ['./forgot-password.component.css']
})
export class ForgotPasswordComponent implements OnInit {
  submitted = signal<boolean>(false);
  success = signal<boolean>(false);
  errorMessage = signal<string>("");

  constructor(private userService: UserService) { }

  forgotForm = new FormGroup({
    email: new FormControl('', [Validators.required, Validators.email]),
  });

  ngOnInit(): void {
  }

  onSubmit() {
    console.warn(this.forgotForm.value);
    this.submitted.set(true);

    if (!this.forgotForm.valid)
      return;

    this.userService
      .resetPassword(this.forgotForm.controls['email'].value || '')
      .subscribe({
        next: () => {
          this.success.set(true);

        },
        error: error => {
          this.success.set(false);
          this.errorMessage = error.error;
        }
      });
  }
}
```

LISTING 14-22: forgot-password.component.ts

Here we have a simple reactive form, with only one form control.

We should add `resetPassword` function in `UserService`:

```
...
  resetPassword(email: string) {
    return this.http
```

```
      .post<User>(`${environment.apiUrl}/auth/reset_password`,
        { email: email }, this.httpOptions);
  }

...
```

LISTING 14-23: user.service.ts

Don't forget to add the respective routing entry in *app-routing.module.ts*.

On the API side, we have the `ResetPassword()` method that works similar to registration, i.e. by sending confirmation code via email. Here, we opt to reuse the RegistrationCode field in User object, as well as the `CreateConfirmationToken()` method.

```
...

  @PostMapping("/reset_password")
  public ResponseEntity<?> resetPassword(@RequestBody ResetEmailDTO resetEmail)
{
    try{
      // Retrieve user by email
      User user = userService.getUserByEmail(resetEmail.getEmail());

      if (user == null) {
        return ResponseEntity.badRequest().body("Email not found");
      }

      // Mark user for password reset and generate a registration code
      user.setStatus("RESET");
      user.setPassword(null);
      user.setRegistrationCode(createConfirmationToken());

      userService.updateUser(user);

      // Send password reset email
      sendPasswordResetEmail(user);

      return ResponseEntity.ok(createDTO(user));
    } catch (Exception e) {
      return ResponseEntity.status(HttpStatus.INTERNAL_SERVER_ERROR)
          .body("Failed to reset password: " + e.getMessage());
    }
  }

...

  private void sendPasswordResetEmail(User user) {
    //Get mail server properties
    Properties props = new Properties();
    props.put("mail.smtp.host", mailConfig.getSmtpHost());
    props.put("mail.smtp.port", mailConfig.getSmtpPort());
```

```java
      props.put("mail.smtp.auth", String.valueOf(mailConfig.isSmtpAuth()));
      props.put("mail.smtp.starttls.enable",
          String.valueOf(mailConfig.isStarttlsEnable()));
      props.put("mail.smtp.ssl.trust", mailConfig.getSslTrust());

      //Create a session with an authenticator
      Session session = Session.getInstance(props, new Authenticator() {
        @Override
        protected PasswordAuthentication getPasswordAuthentication() {
          return new PasswordAuthentication(mailConfig.getSmtpUsername(),
              mailConfig.getSmtpPassword());
        }
      });

      try {
        // Create Message
        Message message = new MimeMessage(session);
        message.setFrom(new InternetAddress("info@my-eshop.com"));
        message.setSubject("Email Reset");
        message.setContent(
            "To insert a new password, please click "
                + " <a href=\"http://localhost:4200/new_password?code="
                + user.getRegistrationCode()
                + "\">here</a>",
            "text/html" //Body is HTML
        );
        message.setRecipient(Message.RecipientType.TO,
            new InternetAddress(user.getEmail()));

        //Send message
        Transport.send(message);
      } catch (MessagingException e) {
        e.printStackTrace();
      }
    }
  }

...
```

LISTING 14-24 AuthController.java

Here is the new class needed for this operation:

```java
package com.example.Eshop.dtos;

import lombok.Data;

@Data
public class ResetEmailDTO {
  private String email;
}
```

LISTING 14-25 ResetEmailDTO.java

Enter new password

Finally, we create the component that will be used, when the user follows the link in the password reset email:

```
<h2>New Password</h2>
<div class="card">
  <div class="card-body" id="cartBody">

    <form [formGroup]="newPasswordForm" (ngSubmit)="onSubmit()">
      <div class="form-row">
        <div class="form-group col-md-2">
          <label for="password">Password:</label>
          <input type="password"
                 formControlName="password"
                 class="form-control form-control-sm"
                 [ngClass]="{ 'is-invalid': submitted() == true &&
newPasswordForm.controls['password'].errors }" />
          @if(newPasswordForm.controls['password'].invalid
          && (newPasswordForm.controls['password'].dirty
          || newPasswordForm.controls['password'].touched)){
          <div class="text-danger">
            @if(newPasswordForm.controls['password'].errors?.['required']){
            <div>
              Password is required
            </div>
            }
          </div>
          }
        </div>
      </div>
      <div class="form-row">
        <div class="form-group col-md-2">
          <label for="confirmPassword">Confirm password:</label>
          <input type="password"
                 formControlName="confirmPassword"
                 class="form-control form-control-sm"
                 [ngClass]="{ 'is-invalid': submitted() == true &&
newPasswordForm.controls['confirmPassword'].errors &&
newPasswordForm.errors?.['passwordsMustMatch'] }" />
          @if((newPasswordForm.controls['confirmPassword'].invalid
          || newPasswordForm.errors?.['passwordsMustMatch'])
          && (newPasswordForm.controls['confirmPassword'].dirty
          || newPasswordForm.controls['confirmPassword'].touched)){
          <div class="text-danger">

@if(newPasswordForm.controls['confirmPassword'].errors?.['required']){
            <div>
              Confirm Password is required
            </div>
            }
            @if(newPasswordForm.errors?.['passwordsMustMatch']){
            <div>
              Passwords must match
            </div>
```

```html
        }
      </div>
      }
    </div>
  </div>
  <button type="submit"
    [disabled]="!newPasswordForm.valid">Change password</button>
  </form>
</div>

@if(success() && submitted()){
<div class="alert alert-success" role="alert">
  Password change was successful<br />
  <button routerLink="/login">Log in</button>
</div>
}

@if(!success() && submitted()){
<div class="alert alert-danger" role="alert">
  {{errorMessage()}}
</div>
}
</div>
```

LISTING 14-26: new-password.component.html

```typescript
import { Component, OnInit, signal } from '@angular/core';
import { FormControl, FormGroup, Validators } from '@angular/forms';
import { ActivatedRoute } from '@angular/router';
import { UserService } from '../../../../app/services/user.service';
import { passwordsMustMatchValidator } from '../../../../app/validators/passwordsMustMatch';

@Component({
  selector: 'app-new-password',
  templateUrl: './new-password.component.html',
  styleUrls: ['./new-password.component.css']
})
export class NewPasswordComponent implements OnInit {

  submitted = signal<boolean>(false);
  success = signal<boolean>(false);
  errorMessage = signal<string>("");
  emailCode = signal<string>("");

  newPasswordForm = new FormGroup({
    password: new FormControl('', Validators.required),
    confirmPassword: new FormControl('', Validators.required),
  }, { validators: [passwordsMustMatchValidator] });

  constructor(
    private route: ActivatedRoute,
    private userService: UserService) { }
```

```
  ngOnInit(): void {
    this.route.queryParams
      .subscribe(params => this.emailCode.set(params['code']));
  }

  onSubmit() {
    this.submitted.set(true);
    if (!this.newPasswordForm.valid)
      return;

    this.userService.changePassword(
      this.newPasswordForm.controls['password'].value || '',
      this.emailCode()
    )
      .subscribe({
        next: () => {
          this.success.set(true);
        },
        error: error => {
          this.success.set(false);
          this.errorMessage = error.error;
        }
      });
  }
}
```

LISTING 14-27: new-password.component.ts

There is not much to see here, just a simple reactive form.

Function `changePassword` should be added in `UserService`:

```
...
  changePassword(newPassword: string, emailCode: string) {
    return this.http
      .post<User>(`${environment.apiUrl}/auth/change_password`,
        { password: newPassword, registrationCode: emailCode },
        this.httpOptions
      );
  }
...
```

LISTING 14-28: user.service.ts

On the API side, we have the following method:

```
...
  @PostMapping("/change_password")
  public ResponseEntity<?> changePassword(@RequestBody User inputUser) {
    try{
      //Get user by registration code
```

```
    User user = userService
        .getUserByRegistrationCode(inputUser.getRegistrationCode());

    if (user == null) {
      return ResponseEntity.badRequest().body("User not found");
    }

    //Hash new password and update user status
    String hashedPassword = passwordEncoder.encode(inputUser.getPassword());
    user.setPassword(hashedPassword);
    user.setStatus("ACTIVE");

    //Generate tokens
    String token = jwtUtilities
        .generateToken(user.getUsername(), user.getId(), user.getRole());
    String refreshToken = jwtUtilities
        .generateRefreshToken(user.getUsername());
    user.setToken(token);
    user.setRefreshToken(refreshToken);
    user.setRefreshTokenExpiry(new Date(System.currentTimeMillis()
        + 1000 * 60 * 60 * 24 * 30));   //30 days expiry

    userService.updateUser(user);   //Save changes

    return ResponseEntity.ok(createDTO(user));
  } catch (Exception e) {
    return ResponseEntity.status(HttpStatus.INTERNAL_SERVER_ERROR)
        .body("Failed to change password: " + e.getMessage());
  }
 }
}
...
```

LISTING 14-29: UserController.cs

Finally, we will add a link to the registration and forgot password pages at the bottom of the login page:

```
...
   <div class="card-body">
     <a routerLink="/register">Register</a> -
     <a routerLink="/forgot_password">Forgot Password</a>
   </div>
...
```

LISTING 14-30: login.component.html

You may want to update the status of the existing users in the Users table to ACTIVE.

You may find the code for this chapter here:

https://github.com/htset/htset-eshop-angular-18-spring/tree/part14

15. Cart in local storage

One important detail with regard to cart functionality is that, when we refresh our page, the cart loses all its contents. That is because the cart is stored in the `StoreService` object and not in permanent storage (like local storage or database). For this reason, we will store the cart contents into Local Storage, so that it will available even after we close and reopen our browser:

```
import { CartItem } from "./cartItem";

export class Cart {
  cartItems: CartItem[] = [];

  constructor(public cartAsJson: string) {
    if (cartAsJson !== '')
      this.cartItems = JSON.parse(cartAsJson) as CartItem[];
  }

  addItem(cartItem: CartItem) {
    let found: boolean = false;
    this.cartItems = this.cartItems.map(ci => {
      if (ci.item?.id == cartItem.item?.id) {
        ci.quantity++;
        found = true;
      }
      return ci;
    });

    if (!found) {
      this.cartItems.push(cartItem);
    }
    this.updateLocalStorage();
  }

  removeItem(item: CartItem) {
    const index = this.cartItems.indexOf(item, 0);
    if (index > -1) {
      this.cartItems.splice(index, 1);
    }
    this.updateLocalStorage();
  }

  emptyCart() {
    this.cartItems = [];
    this.updateLocalStorage();
  }

  getTotalValue(): number {
    let sum = this.cartItems.reduce(
      (a, b) => { a = a + b.item?.price * b.quantity; return a; }, 0);
    return sum;
  }
```

```
  isCartValid(): boolean {
    if   (this.cartItems.find(cartitem   =>   (cartitem.quantity   ==   null   ||
cartitem.quantity <= 0)) === undefined)
      return true;
    return false;
  }

  updateLocalStorage() {
    console.log(JSON.stringify(this.cartItems))
    localStorage.setItem('cart', JSON.stringify(this.cartItems));
  }
}
```

LISTING 15-1: cart.ts

We also update `StoreService` so that it gets the already stored cart contents on initialization:

```
...
private readonly _cart =
  new BehaviorSubject<Cart>(new Cart(localStorage.getItem('cart') || ''));
readonly cart$ = this._cart.asObservable();

get cart(): Cart {
  return this._cart.getValue();
}

set cart(val: Cart) {
  this._cart.next(val);
}
...
```

LISTING 15-2: store.service.ts

Finally, we have to update `CartComponent` so that local storage is updated when we change the quantity of each product:

```
<h3>Cart Details</h3>
<table class="table table-striped">
  <tr>
    <th> </th>
    <th>Name</th>
    <th>Unit Price</th>
    <th>Quantity</th>
    <th>Total Price</th>
    <th> </th>
  </tr>
  @for(item of storeService.cart.cartItems; track item){
  <tr>
    <td>
      <a routerLink="/items/{{item.item.id}}">
        <img src="/angular.svg" width="70px" />
      </a>
```

```html
      </td>
      <td>
        <a routerLink="/items/{{item.item.id}}">
          {{item.item.name}}
        </a>
      </td>
      <td>
        <a routerLink="/items/{{item.item.id}}">
          {{item.item.price}}
        </a>
      </td>
      <td>
        <input type="number" [(ngModel)]="item.quantity"
               (change)="onQuantityChange($event, item.item.id)"
               size="2" id="quantity"
               appAnalytics events="change blur" />
      </td>
      <td>
        <a routerLink="/items/{{item.item.id}}">
          {{item.item.price * item.quantity}}
        </a>
      </td>
      <td>
        <input type="button" (click)="removeFromCart(item)"
               id="remove" value="Remove"
               appAnalytics events="click" />
      </td>
    </tr>
    }
    <tr>
      <td colspan="4"> </td>
      <td>{{storeService.cart.getTotalValue()}}</td>
      <td> </td>
    </tr>
</table>
<br/>
<br/>
<button (click)="emptyCart()" id="empty"
        [disabled]="storeService.cart.cartItems.length == 0"
        appAnalytics events="click">
  Empty Cart
</button>
<br />
<br />
<button routerLink="/checkout" id="checkout"
        [disabled]="storeService.cart.cartItems.length == 0
                  || !storeService.cart.isCartValid()">
  Go to Checkout..
</button>
<br />
<br/>
<button routerLink="">Back to items</button>
<br />
```

LISTING 15-3: cart.component.html

```typescript
import { Component, OnInit } from "@angular/core";
import { CartItem } from "../../../models/cartItem";
import { StoreService } from "../../../services/store.service";

@Component({
  selector: 'app-cart',
  templateUrl: './cart.component.html',
  styleUrls: ['./cart.component.css']
})
export class CartComponent implements OnInit {

  constructor(public storeService: StoreService) { }

  removeFromCart(item: CartItem) {
    this.storeService.cart.removeItem(item);
  }

  emptyCart() {
    this.storeService.cart.emptyCart();
  }

  ngOnInit(): void {
  }

  onQuantityChange(event: any, itemId: number) {
    let newQuantity = parseInt(event.target.value);
    if (Number.isNaN(newQuantity) || newQuantity < 0) {
      newQuantity = 0;
      event.target.value = 0;
    }

    this.storeService.cart.cartItems =
      this.storeService.cart.cartItems.map(item => {
        if (item.item.id === itemId)
          item.quantity = newQuantity;
        return item;
      });
    this.storeService.cart.updateLocalStorage();
  }
}
```

LISTING 15-4: cart.component.ts

Finally, we must update the Payment Component when it uses the Cart object:

```
...
//Submit order
this.orderService.addOrder(order)
  .subscribe((orderResult: Order) => {
    this.storeService.order = orderResult;
    this.storeService.cart.emptyCart();
    this.storeService.deliveryAddress = -1;
```

```
    this.router.navigate(['/summary']);
  });
...
```

LISTING 15-5: payment.component.ts

You may find the code for this chapter here:

https://github.com/htset/htset-eshop-angular-18-spring/tree/part15

16. Admin functionality

In this chapter, we will enhance the administration part of our site, by adding the necessary functionality for administrators to add, remove and modify products. We will also introduce product image uploading functionality, as well as fix the image source path throughout the project.

Backend

This time we will start with the API. The product images will be stored in an external folder (named images) in the backend.

Next, we define a new model describing the product images:

```java
package com.example.Eshop.models;

import com.fasterxml.jackson.annotation.JsonBackReference;
import jakarta.persistence.*;
import lombok.Data;

@Entity
@Data
public class Image {
  @Id
  @GeneratedValue(strategy = GenerationType.IDENTITY)
  private Long id;

  @ManyToOne
  @JoinColumn(name = "item_id", nullable = false)
  @JsonBackReference
  private Item item;

  private String fileName;
  private String fileType;
}
```

LISTING 16-1: Image.java

In an effort to make the API as future-proof as possible, we have chosen to create a new class (Image) that will contain information about the image (or images) associated with a specific product. This way, we will be able to make our frontend display more than one image per product in the future, for instance, in an image gallery.

A simpler alternative would be to add the FileName and FileType information directly into the Item class. However, in our case, we choose to add a list of Image objects to the Item object:

```java
package com.example.Eshop.models;
```

```java
import com.fasterxml.jackson.annotation.JsonManagedReference;
import jakarta.persistence.*;
import lombok.Data;
import java.math.BigDecimal;
import java.util.List;

@Entity
@Data
public class Item {
  @Id
  @GeneratedValue(strategy = GenerationType.IDENTITY)
  private Long id;
  private String name;
  private BigDecimal price;
  private String category;
  private String description;

  @OneToMany(mappedBy = "item", cascade = CascadeType.ALL)
  @JsonManagedReference
  private List<Image> images;
}
```

LISTING 16-2: Item.java

Also, we should create a repository for the images:

```
package com.example.Eshop.repositories;

import com.example.Eshop.models.Image;
import org.springframework.data.jpa.repository.JpaRepository;
import java.util.Optional;

public interface ImageRepository extends JpaRepository<Image, Long> {
  Optional<Image> findByItemId(Long itemId);
}
```

LISTING 16-3: Imagerepository.java

Next we modify the `ItemController` class, in order to add CRUD functionality for our products:

```
package com.example.Eshop.controllers;

import com.example.Eshop.dtos.ItemPayloadDTO;
import com.example.Eshop.models.Item;
import com.example.Eshop.services.ItemService;
import com.example.Eshop.exceptions.ItemNotFoundException;
import org.springframework.http.HttpStatus;
import org.springframework.http.ResponseEntity;
import org.springframework.web.bind.annotation.*;
import org.slf4j.Logger;
import org.slf4j.LoggerFactory;
```

```java
@RestController
@RequestMapping("/items")
public class ItemController {

  private ItemService itemService;
  private final Logger logger = LoggerFactory.getLogger(ItemController.class);

  public ItemController(ItemService itemService){
    this.itemService = itemService;
  }

  @GetMapping
  public ResponseEntity<ItemPayloadDTO> getItems(
      @RequestParam(defaultValue = "0") int pageNumber,
      @RequestParam(defaultValue = "10") int pageSize,
      @RequestParam(required = false) String category,
      @RequestParam(required = false) String name) {
    try {
      //Validate pageNumber and pageSize
      if (pageNumber < 1 || pageSize < 1) {
        return ResponseEntity.badRequest()
            .body(null); //Return 400 Bad Request for invalid page parameters
      }

      ItemPayloadDTO itemPayload = itemService
          .getItems(pageNumber, pageSize, category, name);
      return  ResponseEntity.ok(itemPayload);  //Return  200  OK  with  the  item payload
    } catch (Exception e) {
      logger.error("Error fetching items: {}", e.getMessage());
      return ResponseEntity.status(HttpStatus.INTERNAL_SERVER_ERROR)
          .body(null); //Return 500 Internal Server Error
    }
  }


  @GetMapping("/{id}")
  public ResponseEntity<Item> getItemById(@PathVariable Long id) {
    try {
      Item item = itemService.getItemById(id);
      return ResponseEntity.ok(item); //Return 200 OK with the item
    } catch (ItemNotFoundException e) {
      logger.error("Item not found with id {}: {}", id, e.getMessage());
      return ResponseEntity.status(HttpStatus.NOT_FOUND)
          .body(null); //Return 404 Not Found if the item is not found
    } catch (Exception e) {
      logger.error("Error fetching item by id {}: {}", id, e.getMessage());
      return ResponseEntity.status(HttpStatus.INTERNAL_SERVER_ERROR)
          .body(null); //Return 500 Internal Server Error for other issues
    }
  }

  @PostMapping
  public ResponseEntity<Item> createItem(@RequestBody Item item) {
```

```java
    try {
      Item createdItem = itemService.createItem(item);
      //Return 201 Created with the new item
      return ResponseEntity.status(HttpStatus.CREATED).body(createdItem);
    }
    catch (Exception e) {
      logger.error("Error creating item: {}", e.getMessage());
      //Return 500 Internal Server Error if item creation fails
      return ResponseEntity
          .status(HttpStatus.INTERNAL_SERVER_ERROR).body(null);
    }
  }

  @PutMapping("/{id}")
  public ResponseEntity<Item> updateItem(@PathVariable Long id,
                                          @RequestBody Item updatedItem) {
    try {
      Item item = itemService.updateItem(id, updatedItem);
      //Return 200 OK with the updated item
      return ResponseEntity.ok(item);
    }
    catch (ItemNotFoundException e) {
      logger.error("Error updating item with id {}: {}", id, e.getMessage());
      //Return 404 Not Found if the item to be updated doesn't exist
      return ResponseEntity
          .status(HttpStatus.NOT_FOUND)
          .body(null);
    }
    catch (Exception e) {
      logger.error("Error updating item with id {}: {}", id, e.getMessage());
      //Return 500 Internal Server Error for other issues
      return ResponseEntity
          .status(HttpStatus.INTERNAL_SERVER_ERROR)
          .body(null);
    }
  }

  @DeleteMapping("/{id}")
  public ResponseEntity<Void> deleteItem(@PathVariable Long id) {
    try {
      itemService.deleteItem(id);
      //Return 204 No Content for successful deletion
      return ResponseEntity.noContent().build();
    } catch (ItemNotFoundException e) {
      logger.error("Error deleting item with id {}: {}", id, e.getMessage());
      //Return 404 Not Found if the item doesn't exist
      return ResponseEntity
          .status(HttpStatus.NOT_FOUND).build();
    } catch (Exception e) {
      logger.error("Error deleting item with id {}: {}", id, e.getMessage());
      //Return 500 Internal Server Error for other issues
      return ResponseEntity
          .status(HttpStatus.INTERNAL_SERVER_ERROR).build();
    }
  }
```

}

LISTING 16-4: ItemController.java

We see that we have added the methods for the Add/Edit/Delete functionality. Here are the corresponding methods in `ItemService`:

```
package com.example.Eshop.services;

import com.example.Eshop.dtos.ItemPayloadDTO;
import com.example.Eshop.exceptions.ItemNotFoundException;
import com.example.Eshop.models.Item;
import com.example.Eshop.repositories.ItemRepository;
import org.springframework.data.domain.Page;
import org.springframework.data.domain.PageRequest;
import org.springframework.stereotype.Service;
import org.slf4j.Logger;
import org.slf4j.LoggerFactory;

import java.util.Arrays;
import java.util.List;

@Service
public class ItemService {

  private final ItemRepository itemRepository;
  private static final Logger logger
      = LoggerFactory.getLogger(ItemService.class);

  public ItemService(ItemRepository itemRepository){
    this.itemRepository = itemRepository;
  }

  //Get items based on pagination
  public ItemPayloadDTO getItems(int page, int size, String category,
      String name) {
    try {
      if (page < 1 || size < 1) {
        throw new
            IllegalArgumentException("Page and size must be greater than 0");
      }

      //Split category string into individual categories
      List<String> categories = Arrays.asList(category.split(","));

      Page<Item> itemPage;
      page -= 1; //Pagination starts with 0, in the frontend we start with 1

      if ((category != null && !category.isEmpty())
          || (name != null && !name.isEmpty())) {
        //If search criteria is provided
        itemPage = itemRepository
            .findByColumnContainingValuesAndFilter(categories,
```

```java
              name, PageRequest.of(page, size));
      } else {
        itemPage = itemRepository.findAll(PageRequest.of(page, size));
      }
      return new
          ItemPayloadDTO(itemPage.getContent(), itemPage.getTotalElements());
    } catch (Exception e) {
      logger.error("Error fetching items: {}", e.getMessage());
      throw new RuntimeException("Unable to fetch items, please try again later");
    }
  }

  //Get one item by ID
  public Item getItemById(Long id) {
    try {
      return itemRepository.findById(id)
          .orElseThrow(()
              -> new ItemNotFoundException("Item not found with id: " + id));
    } catch (ItemNotFoundException e) {
      logger.error("Error fetching item by id {}: {}", id, e.getMessage());
      throw e;
    } catch (Exception e) {
      logger.error("Error fetching item by id {}: {}", id, e.getMessage());
      throw new RuntimeException("Unable to fetch item, please try again later");
    }
  }

  //Create a new item
  public Item createItem(Item item) {
    try {
      return itemRepository.save(item);
    }
    catch (Exception e) {
      logger.error("Error creating item: {}", e.getMessage());
      throw new RuntimeException("Unable to create item, please try again later");
    }
  }

  //Update an existing item by ID
  public Item updateItem(Long id, Item updatedItem) {
    try {
      Item existingItem = getItemById(id);
      existingItem.setName(updatedItem.getName());
      existingItem.setDescription(updatedItem.getDescription());
      existingItem.setCategory(updatedItem.getCategory());
      existingItem.setPrice(updatedItem.getPrice());

      return itemRepository.save(existingItem);
    }
    catch (ItemNotFoundException e) {
      logger.error("Error updating item with id {}: {}", id, e.getMessage());
      throw e;
```

```java
    } catch (Exception e) {
      logger.error("Error updating item with id {}: {}", id, e.getMessage());
      throw new RuntimeException("Unable to update item, please try again later");
    }
  }

  //Delete an item by its ID
  public void deleteItem(Long id) {
    try {
      Item item = getItemById(id);
      itemRepository.delete(item);
    }
    catch (ItemNotFoundException e) {
      logger.error("Error deleting item with id {}: {}", id, e.getMessage());
      throw e;
    }
    catch (Exception e) {
      logger.error("Error deleting item with id {}: {}", id, e.getMessage());
      throw new RuntimeException("Unable to delete item, please try again later");
    }
  }
}
```

LISTING 16-5: ItemService.java

Frontend

On the Angular side, we start by creating the corresponding model for the image class:

```typescript
export class Image {
  constructor(
    public itemId: number,
    public fileType: string,
    public fileContent: File,
    public fileName: string
  ) { }
}
```

LISTING 16-6: image.ts

We also add a list of images in the item model:

```typescript
import { Image } from './image'
export interface Item {
  id: number;
  name: string;
  price: number;
  category: string;
```

```
  description?: string;
  images?: Image[];
}
```

LISTING 16-7: item.ts

We proceed with the creation of the AdminItems component, which provides a paginated list of all products. This component is very similar to Items component, available to all users. However, it provides the ability to add a new product or delete or update an existing one. Moreover, it has the form of a grid instead of the cards-based layout viewed by regular users.

```
Page size:
<select [(ngModel)]="storeService.pageSize"
    (change)="onPageSizeChange()" id="pageSize">
  <option value="3">3</option>
  <option value="5">5</option>
  <option value="10">10</option>
  <option value="50">50</option>
</select>
<br />
<button (click)="openFilter()">Filters</button>
<br />
<table class="table table-striped">
  <tr>
    <th>ID</th>
    <th>Name</th>
    <th>Unit Price</th>
    <th>Category</th>
  </tr>
  @for(item of storeService.items; track item.id){
  <tr>
    <td>
      <a routerLink="/admin/item/{{item.id}}">
        @if(item.images !== undefined && item.images[0] !== undefined){
        <img src="{{imageUrl}}/{{item.images[0].fileName}}" height="40px" />
        }
      </a>
    </td>
    <td>
      <a routerLink="/admin/item/{{item.id}}">
        {{item.name}}
      </a>
    </td>
    <td>
      <a routerLink="/admin/item/{{item.id}}">
        {{item.price}}
      </a>
    </td>
    <td>
      <a routerLink="/admin/item/{{item.id}}">
        {{item.category}}
```

```
      </a>
    </td>
    <td><button (click)="delete(item)">Delete</button></td>
  </tr>
  }
</table>

<ngb-pagination [(page)]="storeService.page"
                [pageSize]="storeService.pageSize"
                [collectionSize]="storeService.count"
  (pageChange)="onPageChange($event)">
</ngb-pagination>

<br />
<button routerLink="/admin/new_item">Add new Item</button>
```

LISTING 16-8: admin-items.component.html

```
import { Component, OnInit } from '@angular/core';
import { NgbModal } from '@ng-bootstrap/ng-bootstrap';
import { skip } from 'rxjs/operators';
import { Item } from '../../../../app/models/item';
import { AuthenticationService }
  from '../../../../app/services/authentication.service';
import { ItemService } from '../../../../app/services/item.service';
import { StoreService } from '../../../../app/services/store.service';
import { environment } from '../../../../environments/environment';
import { FilterComponent } from '../../shared/filter/filter.component';

@Component({
  selector: 'app-admin-items',
  templateUrl: './admin-items.component.html',
  styleUrls: ['./admin-items.component.css']
})
export class AdminItemsComponent implements OnInit {

  imageUrl: string = environment.imagesUrl;

  constructor(private itemService: ItemService,
    public storeService: StoreService,
    public authenticationService: AuthenticationService,
    private modalService: NgbModal) { }

  getItems(): void {
    this.itemService
      .getItems(this.storeService.page,
        this.storeService.pageSize, this.storeService.filter)
      .subscribe(itemPayload => {
        this.storeService.items = itemPayload.items;
        this.storeService.count = itemPayload.count;
      });
  }
```

```typescript
  delete(item: Item): void {
    this.itemService.deleteItem(item)
      .subscribe(item => {
        this.storeService.page = 1;
        this.getItems();
      });
  }

  openFilter() {
    this.modalService.open(FilterComponent);
  }

  onPageChange(newPage: number): void {
    this.storeService.page = newPage;
    this.getItems();
  }

  onPageSizeChange(): void {
    this.storeService._pageSizeSubject.next(this.storeService.pageSize);
  }

  ngOnInit(): void {
    this.storeService.pageSizeChanges$
      .subscribe(newPageSize => {
        console.log('new page size:' + this.storeService.pageSize);
        this.storeService.page = 1;
        this.getItems();
      });

    this.storeService.filter$
      .pipe(skip(1))      //skip getting filter at component creation
      .subscribe(newFilter => {
        this.storeService.page = 1;
        this.getItems();
      });

    this.getItems();
  }
}
```

LISTING 16-9: admin-items.component.ts

We proceed with updating the ItemService, so that it provides functions for inserting new items as well as updating and deleting existing ones:

```typescript
import { Injectable, } from '@angular/core';
import { Observable, catchError, of } from 'rxjs';
import { Item } from '../models/item';
import { ItemPayload } from '../models/itemPayload';
import { Filter } from '../models/filter';
import { HttpClient, HttpHeaders, HttpParams } from '@angular/common/http';
import { environment } from '../../environments/environment';
```

```typescript
@Injectable({
  providedIn: 'root'
})
export class ItemService {

  itemsUrl = `${environment.apiUrl}/items`;

  httpOptions = {
    headers: new HttpHeaders({ 'Content-Type': 'application/json' })
  };

  getItems(page: number, pageSize: number, filter: Filter)
    : Observable<ItemPayload> {
    let categoriesString: string = "";
    filter.categories
      .forEach(cc => categoriesString = categoriesString + cc + "#");
    if (categoriesString.length > 0)
      categoriesString = categoriesString
        .substring(0, categoriesString.length - 1);

    let params = new HttpParams()
      .set("name", filter.name)
      .set("pageNumber", page.toString())
      .set("pageSize", pageSize.toString())
      .set("category", categoriesString);

    return this.http.get<ItemPayload>(this.itemsUrl, { params: params });
  }

  getItem(id: number): Observable<Item> {
    const url = `${this.itemsUrl}/${id}`;
    return this.http.get<Item>(url);
  }

  updateItem(item: Item): Observable<Item> {
    const id = item.id;
    const url = `${this.itemsUrl}/${id}`;

    return this.http.put<Item>(url, item, this.httpOptions);
  }

  addItem(item: Item): Observable<Item> {
    return this.http.post<Item>(this.itemsUrl, item, this.httpOptions);
  }

  deleteItem(item: Item | number): Observable<Item> {
    const id = typeof item === 'number' ? item : item.id;
    const url = `${this.itemsUrl}/${id}`;

    return this.http.delete<Item>(url, this.httpOptions);
  }

  constructor(private http: HttpClient) { }
}
```

LISTING 16-10: item.service.ts

Then, we proceed by creating the `AdminItemForm` component. This component will be used by admins to edit the details of a product, as well as upload a new image for the product. Adding a new product is a two-step process; first we create and save the new product, then we upload its picture.

Note that, for educational purposes, this time we choose to create a template-driven form, instead of a reactive one:

```
<div class="container">
  <div style="width:50%;float:left;">
    <h3>{{item().name}}</h3>
    <form (ngSubmit)="onSubmit()" #itemForm="ngForm">
      <div class="form-group col-md-4">
        <label for="id">ID</label>
        <input type="text" class="form-control form-control-sm"
          id="id" readonly [(ngModel)]="item().id" name="id"
          #id="ngModel">
      </div>

      <div class="form-group col-md-8">
        <label for="name">Name</label>
        <input type="text" class="form-control form-control-sm"
          id="name" required [(ngModel)]="item().name" name="name"
          #name="ngModel">

        @if(name.invalid && (name.dirty || name.touched)){
        <div class="alert alert-danger">Name is required</div>
        }
      </div>

      <div class="form-group col-md-4">
        <label for="price">Price</label>
        <input type="text" class="form-control form-control-sm"
          id="price" required
          [ngClass]="{ 'is-invalid':  item().price <= 0 }"
          [(ngModel)]="item().price" name="price" #price="ngModel">

        @if(price.invalid && (price.dirty || price.touched)){
        <div class="alert alert-danger">Price is required</div>
        }
        @if(price.value <= 0 && (price.dirty || price.touched)){
          <div class="alert alert-danger">Price must be greater than zero</div>
        }
      </div>

      <div class="form-group col-md-8">
        <label for="description">Description</label>
        <textarea class="form-control form-control-sm" id="description"
            [(ngModel)]="item().description" name="description">
            </textarea>
```

```html
    </div>

    <div class="form-group col-md-8">
      <label for="category">Item category</label>
      <select class="form-control form-control-sm" id="category"
        required [(ngModel)]="item().category" name="category"
        #category="ngModel">
        @for(cat of categories; track cat){
        <option [value]="cat">{{cat}}</option>
        }
      </select>
      @if(category.invalid && (category.dirty || category.touched)){
      <div class="alert alert-danger">Category is required</div>
      }
    </div>

    <div class="form-group col-md-8">
      <button type="submit" id="submit"
        [disabled]="!itemForm.form.valid || itemForm.form.pristine">
        Save
      </button>
      <button type="button" id="back" (click)="goBack()">Back</button>
    </div>
  </form>

  @if(success() && submitted()){
  <div class="alert alert-success" role="alert">Item was saved</div>
  }
  @if(!success() && submitted()){
  <div class="alert alert-danger" role="alert">Item was not saved</div>
  }

</div>

@if(item().id > 0){
<div style="width:50%; float:left;vertical-align: middle;">
  @if(imageLink() !== undefined){
  <img [src]="imageLink()" alt="product image" style="border-style: solid;" />
  }
  @else {
  No picture yet
  }
  <div class="row" style="margin-bottom:15px;">
    <div class="col-md-3">
      <input #imageInput type="file" #file placeholder="Choose file"
        (change)="processFile(imageInput)"
        style="display:none;">
      <button type="button" class="btn btn-success" (click)="file.click()">
        Upload File
      </button>
    </div>
    <div class="col-md-4">
      <span class="upload" *ngIf="progress() > 0">
        {{progress()}}%
      </span>
```

```html
      <span class="upload" *ngIf="message()">
        {{message()}}
      </span>
    </div>
  </div>
</div>
}
</div>
```

LISTING 16-11: admin-item-form.component.html

```typescript
import { Component, OnInit, ViewChild, signal } from '@angular/core';
import { NgForm } from '@angular/forms';
import { ActivatedRoute, Router } from '@angular/router';
import { Item } from '../../../../app/models/item';
import { ItemService } from '../../../../app/services/item.service';
import { Location } from '@angular/common';
import { HttpEventType } from '@angular/common/http';
import { environment } from '../../../../environments/environment';
import { ImageService } from '../../../../app/services/image.service';
import { Image } from '../../../../app/models/image';

@Component({
  selector: 'app-admin-item-form',
  templateUrl: './admin-item-form.component.html',
  styleUrls: ['./admin-item-form.component.css']
})
export class AdminItemFormComponent implements OnInit {

  @ViewChild('itemForm') public itemForm?: NgForm;
  categories: string[] = ["", "Shoes", "Clothes", "Glasses", "Gear"];
  mode = signal<string>("new");
  item = signal<Item>({ id: 0, name: "", price: 0,
                category: "", description: "" });
  public progress = signal<number>(0);
  public message = signal<string>('');
  success = signal<boolean>(false);
  submitted = signal<boolean>(false);
  imageLink = signal<string | undefined>('');
  image?: Image;

  constructor(
    private route: ActivatedRoute,
    public itemService: ItemService,
    private location: Location,
    private router: Router,
    private imageService: ImageService
  ) { }

  ngOnInit(): void {
    this.getItem();
  }
```

```typescript
onSubmit(): void {
  if (this.item().id > 0) {
    this.itemService.updateItem(this.item())
      .subscribe({
        next: () => {
          this.itemForm?.form.markAsPristine();
          this.success.set(true);
          this.submitted.set(true);
        },
        error: () => {
          this.success.set(false);
          this.submitted.set(true);
        }
      });
  }
  else {
    this.itemService.addItem(this.item())
      .subscribe((item) => {
        this.item.set(item);
        this.itemForm?.form.markAsPristine();
      });
  }
}

getItem(): void {
  if (this.route.snapshot.paramMap.get('id') === 'undefined'
    || this.route.snapshot.paramMap.get('id') === null
    || Number(this.route.snapshot.paramMap.get('id')) === 0) {

    this.item.set({ id: 0, name: "", price: 0,
                    category: "", description: "" });
  }
  else {
    const id = Number(this.route.snapshot.paramMap.get('id'));
    if (id > 0) {
      this.itemService.getItem(id)
        .subscribe((item) => {
          this.item.set(item);
          let imagesArray = this.item()?.images;
          if (imagesArray !== undefined
            && imagesArray[0]?.fileName !== undefined)
            this.imageLink.set(`${environment.imagesUrl}/`
              + imagesArray[0]?.fileName + '?' + Math.random());
          else
            this.imageLink.set(undefined);
        });
    }
    else {
      this.router.navigate(['/404']);
    }
  }
}

goBack(): void {
```

```
    this.location.back();
  }

  processFile(imageInput: any) {
    const file: File = imageInput.files[0];
    const reader = new FileReader();

    reader.addEventListener('load', (event: any) => {
      let fileExtension = file.name.split('?')[0].split('.').pop();
      this.image = new Image(this.item().id,
        file.type, file, this.item().id.toString() + '.' + fileExtension);

      this.imageService.upload(this.image)
        .subscribe(event => {
          if (event.type === HttpEventType.UploadProgress)
            this.progress.set(
                Math.round(100 * event.loaded / (event.total || 1)));
          else if (event.type === HttpEventType.Response) {
            this.message.set('Upload success.');
            this.updateImageLink();
          }
        });
    });
    reader.readAsDataURL(file);
  }

  public updateImageLink() {
    this.imageLink.set(`${environment.imagesUrl}/`
      + this.image?.fileName + '?' + Math.random());
  }
}
```

LISTING 16-12: admin-item-form.component.ts

When the user chooses to add a new image for this item, the `processFile()` function is called. This function creates a new `Image` object that contains the actual image, along with image file information and sends it to the backend via the `ImageService`. Tha same function also shows the progress of the uploading as a percentage.

Here is the code for the `ImageService`:

```
import { HttpClient, HttpEvent } from '@angular/common/http';
import { Injectable } from '@angular/core';
import { Observable } from 'rxjs';
import { environment } from '../../environments/environment';
import { Image } from '../../app/models/image';

@Injectable({
    providedIn: 'root'
})
export class ImageService {
```

```
    constructor(private http: HttpClient) { }

    public upload(image: Image): Observable<HttpEvent<Response>> {
        const formData = new FormData();

        formData.append('image', image.fileContent, image.fileName);
        formData.append('id', image.itemId.toString());
        return this.http.post<Response>(`${environment.apiUrl}/images`,
            formData, { reportProgress: true, observe: 'events' });
    }

    public getImage(itemId: number): Observable<Image> {
        return this.http.get<Image>(`${environment.apiUrl}/images/${itemId}`);
    }
}
```

LISTING 16-13: image.service.ts

The `ImageService` calls the `${environment.apiUrl}/image` URL in the backend. We will create the respective controller later in this chapter.

Let's not forget to add the routing entries:

```
...
  {
    path: 'admin', component: AdminHomeComponent,
    canActivate: [AuthGuard],
    children: [
      {
        path: 'users',
        component: AdminUsersComponent,
        canActivate: [AuthGuard]
      },
      {
        path: 'items',
        component: AdminItemsComponent,
        canActivate: [AuthGuard]
      },
      {
        path: 'item/:id',
        component: AdminItemFormComponent,
        canActivate: [AuthGuard]
      },
      {
        path: 'new_item',
        component: AdminItemFormComponent,
        canActivate: [AuthGuard]
      }
    ]
  },
...
```

LISTING 16-14: app-routing.module.ts

The routes are children of the admin route; for example, the items route will be called as `admin/items`.

We also add the link to the admin version of item catalog:

```html
<h2>Admin pages</h2>
<nav class="navbar navbar-expand-lg navbar-light bg-light">
  <div class="container-fluid">
    <ul class="navbar-nav">
      <li class="nav-item">
        <a class="nav-link"
           routerLink="/admin/users">Users </a>
      </li>
      <li class="nav-item">
        <a class="nav-link"
           routerLink="/admin/items">Items </a>
      </li>
    </ul>
  </div>
</nav>
<router-outlet></router-outlet>
```

LISTING 16-15: admin-home.component.html

Finally, we should add the URL for the images folder in the environments files:

```
export const environment = {
  production: false,
  apiUrl: 'http://localhost:8080',
  imagesUrl: 'http://localhost:8080/images'
};
```

LISTING 16-16: environment.development.ts

```
export const environment = {
  production: true,
  apiUrl: 'http://localhost:8080',
  imagesUrl: 'http://localhost:8080/images'
};
```

LISTING 16-17: environment.ts

Backend (again)

Now, we return to backend in order to create the controller for the `${environment.apiUrl}/images` URL:

```java
package com.example.Eshop.controllers;

import com.example.Eshop.models.Image;
import com.example.Eshop.models.Item;
import com.example.Eshop.repositories.ImageRepository;
import com.example.Eshop.repositories.ItemRepository;
import org.springframework.http.HttpStatus;
import org.springframework.http.ResponseEntity;
import org.springframework.web.bind.annotation.PostMapping;
import org.springframework.web.bind.annotation.RequestMapping;
import org.springframework.web.bind.annotation.RequestParam;
import org.springframework.web.bind.annotation.RestController;
import org.springframework.web.multipart.MultipartFile;
import java.io.IOException;
import java.io.InputStream;
import java.nio.file.Files;
import java.nio.file.Path;
import java.nio.file.Paths;
import java.nio.file.StandardCopyOption;
import java.util.Collections;

@RestController
@RequestMapping("/images")
public class ImageController {
  private static String IMAGES_FOLDER = "C://images";

  private final ImageRepository imageRepository;
  private final ItemRepository itemRepository;

  ImageController(ImageRepository repository,
                  ItemRepository itemRepository) {
    this.imageRepository = repository;
    this.itemRepository = itemRepository;
  }

  @PostMapping
  public   ResponseEntity<?>   imageUpload(@RequestParam("image")   MultipartFile file) {

    try{
      if (file.isEmpty()) {
        return ResponseEntity.badRequest().body("Image is empty");
      }

      Path pathToSave = Paths.get(IMAGES_FOLDER);
      String originalFileName = file.getOriginalFilename();
      String fileName = originalFileName != null ? originalFileName.trim() : "uploaded_image";
      Path fullPath = pathToSave.resolve(fileName);
      String dbPath = IMAGES_FOLDER + "/" + fileName;

      try (InputStream inputStream = file.getInputStream()) {
        Files.copy(inputStream, fullPath, StandardCopyOption.REPLACE_EXISTING);
      }
```

```java
        //Parse item ID and image type from file name
        Long         itemId         =         Long.parseLong(fileName.substring(0, fileName.indexOf('.')));
        String fileType = fileName.substring(fileName.indexOf('.') + 1);

        Item item = itemRepository.findById(itemId)
            .orElseThrow(() -> new RuntimeException("Item not found"));

        //Find or create an Image entity in the database
        Image image = imageRepository.findByItemId(itemId).orElse(new Image());
        image.setItem(item);
        image.setFileName(fileName);
        image.setFileType(fileType);

        //Save or update the image entity
        imageRepository.save(image);

        return ResponseEntity.ok(Collections.singletonMap("dbPath", dbPath));

    } catch (IOException e) {
      return ResponseEntity.status(HttpStatus.INTERNAL_SERVER_ERROR)
          .body("Failed to upload the file: " + e.getMessage());
    }
  }
}
```

LISTING 16-18: ImagesController.cs

We need to configure Spring Boot so that it is aware of the location of the images folder. We also must declare the types of images that will be accepted. This is performed in WebConfig class:

```java
package com.example.Eshop.config;

import org.springframework.context.annotation.Configuration;
import org.springframework.http.MediaType;
import org.springframework.web.servlet.config.annotation.ContentNegotiationConfigurer;
import org.springframework.web.servlet.config.annotation.ResourceHandlerRegistry;
import org.springframework.web.servlet.config.annotation.WebMvcConfigurer;

@Configuration
public class WebConfig implements WebMvcConfigurer {

  @Override
  public void addResourceHandlers(ResourceHandlerRegistry registry) {
    registry.addResourceHandler("/images/**")
        .addResourceLocations("file:///c:/images/");
  }

  @Override
  public void configureContentNegotiation(
```

```
        ContentNegotiationConfigurer configurer) {
    configurer.defaultContentType(MediaType.APPLICATION_OCTET_STREAM);
    configurer.mediaType("svg", MediaType.valueOf("image/svg+xml"))
        .mediaType("png", MediaType.IMAGE_PNG)
        .mediaType("jpg", MediaType.IMAGE_JPEG)
        .mediaType("jpeg", MediaType.IMAGE_JPEG)
        .mediaType("gif", MediaType.IMAGE_GIF);
  }
}
```

LISTING 16-19: WebConfig.java

Finally, we must permit access to the images folder in SecurityConfig:

```
@Bean
public SecurityFilterChain securityFilterChain(HttpSecurity http)
    throws Exception {
  http
      //Disable CSRF since this is a stateless REST API
      .csrf(csrf -> csrf.disable())
      //Enable CORS
      .cors(cors -> cors.configurationSource(corsConfigurationSource()))
      //Define public endpoints that can be accessed without authentication
      .authorizeHttpRequests(auth -> auth
              .requestMatchers("/users/**").hasRole("ADMIN")
              .requestMatchers(
                  "/auth/**",
                  "/items/**",
                  "/images/**",
                  "/remoteLogging/**").permitAll()   // Allow access to auth endpoints
              .anyRequest().authenticated()   // All other endpoints get authentication
      )
      //Add JWT token filter before UsernamePasswordAuthenticationFilter
      .addFilterBefore(jwtRequestFilter,
          UsernamePasswordAuthenticationFilter.class);

  return http.build();
}
```

LISTING 16-20: SecurityConfig.java

One more thing...

Now that we have a new place to get the images from, we should update the respective components that display the items list and the item details to the customers (i.e. ItemsComponent and ItemsDetailsComponent classes). The code is almost the same as the one we used for the Admin components and you can find it in the GitHub repository below:

https://github.com/htset/htset-eshop-angular-18-spring/tree/part16

17. Order processing

In this chapter we will complete the web store functionality, by creating the admin pages needed for order processing.

Backend

Instead of providing a RESTful endpoint, as we did for the items list, here we will use *GraphQL*. GraphQL is a query language for APIs that allows clients to request exactly the data they need, making it efficient and flexible compared to traditional REST APIs. It enables clients to specify queries for nested and related data in a single request, minimizing the need for multiple roundtrips to the server.

First of all, we have to install the necessary dependencies in Maven:

```xml
<dependency>
  <groupId>org.springframework.boot</groupId>
  <artifactId>spring-boot-starter-graphql</artifactId>
</dependency>
<dependency>
  <groupId>com.graphql-java</groupId>
  <artifactId>graphql-java-extended-scalars</artifactId>
  <version>22.0</version>
</dependency>
```

LISTING 17-1: pom.xml

The second dependency will be used to support `BigDecimal` in GraphQL.

Then, we proceed with adding GET functionality in the `OrderController`:

```java
package com.example.Eshop.controllers;

import com.example.Eshop.dtos.OrderDTO;
import com.example.Eshop.dtos.OrderPayloadDTO;
import com.example.Eshop.models.Order;
import com.example.Eshop.services.OrderService;
import org.springframework.graphql.data.method.annotation.Argument;
import org.springframework.graphql.data.method.annotation.QueryMapping;
import org.springframework.http.HttpStatus;
import org.springframework.http.ResponseEntity;
import org.springframework.web.bind.annotation.*;
import jakarta.validation.Valid;

import java.util.List;
import java.util.Optional;

@RestController
@RequestMapping("/orders")
public class OrderController {
```

```java
  private final OrderService orderService;

  public OrderController(OrderService orderService) {
    this.orderService = orderService;
  }

  @PostMapping
  public ResponseEntity<OrderDTO> postOrder(@Valid @RequestBody OrderDTO dto) {
    try {
      OrderDTO createdOrder = orderService.createOrder(dto);
      return ResponseEntity.status(HttpStatus.CREATED).body(createdOrder);
    } catch (Exception e) {
      return ResponseEntity.status(HttpStatus.BAD_REQUEST).build();
    }
  }

  @QueryMapping
  public OrderPayloadDTO getOrders(@Argument int page,
                                  @Argument int pageSize,
                                  @Argument String search) {
    List<Order> orders
        = orderService.findPaginatedOrders(page -1, pageSize, search);
    int totalCount = orderService.getTotalOrderCount(search);

    OrderPayloadDTO response = new OrderPayloadDTO();
    response.setOrders(orders);
    response.setTotalCount(totalCount);

    return response;
  }

  @GetMapping("/{id}")
  public ResponseEntity<OrderDTO> getOrder(@PathVariable Long id) {
    Optional<OrderDTO> orderDTO = orderService.getOrderById(id);
    return orderDTO.map(ResponseEntity::ok)
        .orElseGet(() -> ResponseEntity.status(HttpStatus.NOT_FOUND).build());
  }
}
```
LISTING 17-2: OrderController.java

Here is the OrderService class:

...

```java
  public List<Order> findPaginatedOrders(int page, int pageSize, String search)
{
    Pageable pageable = PageRequest.of(page, pageSize);
    if(search == null || search.isEmpty())
      return orderRepository.findAll(pageable).getContent();
    else
      return orderRepository.findAllBySearchCriteria(search, pageable);
  }
```

```
  public int getTotalOrderCount(String search) {
    if(search == null || search.isEmpty())
      return orderRepository.countAll();
    else
      return orderRepository.countBySearchCriteria(search);
  }

  public Optional<OrderDTO> getOrderById(Long id) {
    return orderRepository.findById(id).map(this::createDTOFromOrder);
  }

...
```
LISTING 17-3: OrderService.java

In the controller, we have added two methods:

- getOrders() for retrieving all orders
- getOrder() to get an order by its ID

The important stuff here is getOrders(), which we have annotated with the @QueryMapping annotation. This method returns an OrderPayloadDTO object, which (like ItemPayloadDTO) is used to enable pagination:

```
package com.example.Eshop.dtos;
import com.example.Eshop.models.Order;
import lombok.Data;

import java.util.List;

@Data
public class OrderPayloadDTO {
  private int totalCount; //Total number of orders matching the criteria
  private List<Order> orders; //List of paginated orders
}
```

LISTING 17-4: OrderPayloadDTO.java

Next, we need to create the GraphQL schema that will be used to retrieve the paginated list of orders. We will create a new folder (graphql) inside the resources folder of our project. Inside this new folder we will create a schema file (*schema.graphqls*):

```
scalar BigDecimal

type OrderDetail {
    id: ID!
    orderId: ID!
    productId: ID!
    quantity: Int!
    price: BigDecimal!
}
```

```
type Order {
    id: ID!
    userId: ID!
    orderDate: String!
    totalPrice: BigDecimal!
    orderDetails: [OrderDetail!]!
    firstName: String!
    lastName: String!
    street: String!
    zip: String!
    city: String!
    country: String!
}

type OrderPayloadDTO {
    totalCount: Int!
    orders: [Order!]!
}

type Query {
    getOrders(page: Int, pageSize: Int, search: String): OrderPayloadDTO
}
```

LISTING 17-5: OrderPayloadDTO.java

This GraphQL schema defines the Order, OrderDetail and OrderPayloadDTO types that describe the order information. It also defines the getOrders query that will be called by the GraphQL client (frontend).

Finally, we have to add yet another configuration file (in the config package of course), this time for GraphQL:

```
package com.example.Eshop.config;

import graphql.scalars.ExtendedScalars;
import org.springframework.context.annotation.Bean;
import org.springframework.context.annotation.Configuration;
import org.springframework.graphql.execution.RuntimeWiringConfigurer;

@Configuration
public class GraphQlConfig {

  @Bean
  public RuntimeWiringConfigurer runtimeWiringConfigurer() {
    return wiringBuilder -> wiringBuilder
        .scalar(ExtendedScalars.GraphQLBigDecimal);

  }
}
```

LISTING 17-6: GraphQlConfig.java

This is used to configure a custom scalar (big decimal) type in our Spring Boot application.

Frontend

We start by installing the Apollo GraphQL client in our project:

```
npm install @apollo/client @angular/core apollo-angular graphql
```

We proceed by creating the component that displays all submitted orders.

```
Page size:
<select [(ngModel)]="storeService.orderPageSize"
        (change)="onPageSizeChange()" id="pageSize">
  <option value="3">3</option>
  <option value="5">5</option>
  <option value="10">10</option>
  <option value="50">50</option>
</select>
<br />
Search:
<input type="text" [(ngModel)]="search"
       (keyup)="onSearchChange($event)" />
<br />
<table class="table table-striped">
  <tr>
    <th>ID</th>
    <th>Name</th>
    <th>City</th>
    <th>Date</th>
    <th>Price</th>
  </tr>

  @for(order of storeService.orders; track order){
  <tr>
    <td>
      <a routerLink="/admin/order/{{order.id}}">
        {{order.id}}
      </a>
    </td>
    <td>
      <a routerLink="/admin/order/{{order.id}}">
        {{order.firstName + ' ' + order.lastName}}
      </a>
    </td>
    <td>
      <a routerLink="/admin/order/{{order.id}}">
        {{order.city}}
      </a>
    </td>
    <td>
      <a routerLink="/admin/order/{{order.id}}">
```

```html
      {{order.orderDate | date:'short':'IST'}}
    </a>
  </td>
  <td>
    <a routerLink="/admin/order/{{order.id}}">
      {{order.totalPrice}}
    </a>
  </td>
</tr>
}
</table>

<ngb-pagination [(page)]="storeService.orderPage"
                [pageSize]="storeService.orderPageSize"
                [collectionSize]="storeService.orderCount"
                (pageChange)="onPageChange($event)">
</ngb-pagination>
```

LISTING 17-7: admin-orders.component.html

```typescript
import { Component, OnInit } from '@angular/core';
import { AuthenticationService } from '../../../services/authentication.service';
import { OrderService } from '../../../services/order.service';
import { StoreService } from '../../../services/store.service';

@Component({
  selector: 'app-admin-orders',
  templateUrl: './admin-orders.component.html',
  styleUrls: ['./admin-orders.component.css']
})
export class AdminOrdersComponent implements OnInit {

  search: string = "";

  constructor(private orderService: OrderService,
    public storeService: StoreService,
    public authenticationService: AuthenticationService) { }

  getOrders(): void {
    this.orderService
      .getOrders(this.storeService.orderPage,
        this.storeService.orderPageSize, this.search)
      .subscribe(orders => {
        this.storeService.orders = orders.data.getOrders.orders;
        this.storeService.orderCount = orders.data.getOrders.totalCount;
      });
  }

  onPageChange(newPage: number): void {
    this.storeService.orderPage = newPage;
    this.getOrders();
  }
```

```typescript
  onPageSizeChange(): void {
    this.storeService.orderPageSize = Number(this.storeService.orderPageSize);
    this.storeService._orderPageSizeSubject
      .next(this.storeService.orderPageSize);
  }

  ngOnInit(): void {
    this.storeService.orderPageSizeChanges$
      .subscribe(newPageSize => {
        this.storeService.orderPage = 1;
        this.getOrders();
      });

    this.getOrders();
  }

  onSearchChange(event: any) {
    this.getOrders();
  }
}
```

LISTING 17-8: admin-orders.component.ts

This component also enables admin users to search orders regarding first name, last name and city, by using the search text input.

Next, we create another component that will display detailed information about each order:

```html
<h3>{{order.firstName + ' ' + order.lastName}}</h3>
<div>
  <div class="row">
    <div class="col-md-6">Order Date:
        {{order.orderDate | date:'short':'IST'}}</div>
  </div>
  <div class="row">
    <div class="col-md-6">Total Price: {{order.totalPrice}}</div>
  </div>
  <div class="row">
    <div class="col-md-6">Address:
        {{order.street + ' ,' + order.zip + ' '
            + order.city + ', ' + order.country}}</div>
  </div>
</div>
<div>
  <table class="table">
    <thead>
      <tr>
        <th>Item Name</th>
        <th>Quantity</th>
        <th>Unit Price</th>
        <th>Total Price</th>
      </tr>
```

```html
    </thead>
    <tbody>
      @for(details of order.orderDetails; track details){
      <tr>
        <td>
          {{details.itemName}}
        </td>
        <td>
          {{details.quantity}}
        </td>
        <td>
          {{details.itemUnitPrice}}
        </td>
        <td>
          {{details.totalPrice}}
        </td>
      </tr>
      }
    </tbody>
  </table>
</div>
<div class="row">
  <div class="col-md-3">
    <button routerLink="/admin/orders">Back to orders</button>
  </div>
</div>
```

LISTING 17-9: admin-order-details.component.html

```typescript
import { Component, OnInit } from '@angular/core';
import { ActivatedRoute } from '@angular/router';
import { Order } from '../../../../app/models/order';
import { OrderService } from '../../../services/order.service';

@Component({
  selector: 'app-admin-order-details',
  templateUrl: './admin-order-details.component.html',
  styleUrls: ['./admin-order-details.component.css']
})
export class AdminOrderDetailsComponent implements OnInit {

  order: Order = { id: 0 };

  constructor(private route: ActivatedRoute,
    private orderService: OrderService) { }

  getOrder(): void {
    const id = Number(this.route.snapshot.paramMap.get('id'));
    this.orderService
      .getOrder(id)
      .subscribe(order => {
        this.order = order;
      });
  }
```

```
  ngOnInit(): void {
    this.getOrder();
  }
}
```

LISTING 17-10: admin-order-details.component.ts

Both components make use of the OrderService:

```
import { HttpClient, HttpHeaders } from '@angular/common/http';
import { Injectable } from '@angular/core';
import { Order } from '../models/order';
import { environment } from '../../environments/environment';
import { Observable } from 'rxjs';
import { Apollo, gql } from 'apollo-angular';

@Injectable({
  providedIn: 'root'
})
export class OrderService {

  httpOptions = {
    headers: new HttpHeaders({ 'Content-Type': 'application/json' })
  };

  constructor(private http: HttpClient,
    private apollo: Apollo) { }

  addOrder(order: Order) {
    return this.http
      .post<Order>(`${environment.apiUrl}/orders`, order);
  }

  getOrders(page: number, pageSize: number, search?: string): Observable<any> {
    return this.apollo.query({
      query: gql`
        query getOrders($page: Int, $pageSize: Int, $search: String) {
          getOrders(page: $page, pageSize: $pageSize, search: $search) {
            totalCount
            orders{
              id
              userId
              orderDate
              totalPrice
              firstName
              lastName
            }
          }
        }
      `,
      variables: {
        page,
```

```
      pageSize,
      search: search || null, // Pass null if no search term is provided
    },
  });
}

getOrder(orderId: number): Observable<Order> {
  return this.http
    .get<Order>(`${environment.apiUrl}/orders/${orderId}`);
}
}
```

LISTING 17-11: order.service.ts

We see here that in getOrders function we make a GraphQl query using Apollo.

Since this pagination component is separate from the one in the items list component, we must define its own variables in StoreService:

```
...
private readonly _orders = new BehaviorSubject<Order[]>([]);
readonly orders$ = this._orders.asObservable();

get orders(): Order[] {
return this._orders.getValue();
}

set orders(val: Order[]) {
this._orders.next(val);
}

private readonly _orderPage = new BehaviorSubject<number>(1);
readonly orderPage$ = this._orderPage.asObservable();

get orderPage(): number {
return this._orderPage.getValue();
}

set orderPage(val: number) {
this._orderPage.next(val);
}

public orderPageSize: number = 3;
public readonly _orderPageSizeSubject = new Subject<number>();
public orderPageSizeChanges$ = this._orderPageSizeSubject.asObservable();

private readonly _orderCount = new BehaviorSubject<number>(1);
readonly orderCount$ = this._orderCount.asObservable();

get orderCount(): number {
return this._orderCount.getValue();
}
```

```
set orderCount(val: number) {
  this._orderCount.next(val);
}
...
```

LISTING 17-12: store.service.ts

Let's not forget to add the routing entries:

```
...
{
  path: 'orders',
  component: AdminOrdersComponent,
  canActivate: [AuthGuard]
},
{
  path: 'order/:id',
  component: AdminOrderDetailsComponent,
  canActivate: [AuthGuard]
}
...
```

LISTING 17-13: app-routing.module.ts

Also, we add a new menu entry at admin home:

```
<h2>Admin pages</h2>
<nav class="navbar navbar-expand-lg navbar-light bg-light">
  <div class="container-fluid">
    <ul class="navbar-nav">
      <li class="nav-item">
        <a class="nav-link"
           routerLink="/admin/users">Users </a>
      </li>
      <li class="nav-item">
        <a class="nav-link"
           routerLink="/admin/items">Items </a>
      </li>
      <li class="nav-item">
        <a class="nav-link"
           routerLink="/admin/orders">Orders </a>
      </li>
    </ul>
  </div>
</nav>
<router-outlet></router-outlet>
```

LISTING 17-14: admin-home.component.html

Finally, we have to add Apollo to our *app.module.ts* file:

```
...
import { ApolloModule, APOLLO_OPTIONS } from 'apollo-angular';
import { HttpLink } from 'apollo-angular/http';
import { InMemoryCache } from '@apollo/client/core';

@NgModule({
  imports: [
...
    ApolloModule
  ],
  providers: [
...
    {
      provide: APOLLO_OPTIONS,
      useFactory: (httpLink: HttpLink) => {
        return {
          cache: new InMemoryCache(),
          link: httpLink.create({
            uri: 'http://localhost:8080/graphql',  // our GraphQL endpoint
          }),
        };
      },
      deps: [HttpLink],
    }
  ],
...
```

LISTING 17-15: app.module.ts

There are many things we could do with order processing, like editing the order details, toggling the order's state, and so on. This is left as an exercise to the reader.

You may find the code for this chapter in GitHub:

https://github.com/htset/htset-eshop-angular-18-spring/tree/part17

18. Angular testing – part 1

In this chapter, we will introduce unit testing capabilities to our web application. Unit testing is essential during development, as it makes us fell more assured that our app works as expected.

We will start by running all the tests that have been automatically generated by the Angular CLI, when we created the components and the services of our web site:

```
ng test
```

We will see that almost all tests fail. That's because in the components and the services that we have written so far, we have made extensive use of the `HttpClient` and `Router` modules. When we create the testbed to run our unit tests, we have to import the respective test modules.

For example, in the `ItemDetailsComponent` test spec, before running each test, we have to import those references:

```
beforeEach(async () => {
  await TestBed.configureTestingModule({
    declarations: [ItemDetailsComponent],
    imports: [RouterModule.forRoot([])],
    providers: [
      provideHttpClient(),
      provideHttpClientTesting()
    ]
  })
  .compileComponents();

  fixture = TestBed.createComponent(ItemDetailsComponent);
  component = fixture.componentInstance;
  fixture.detectChanges();
});
```

LISTING 18-1: item-details.component.spec.ts

For services, we will have to add the following providers:

```
beforeEach(() => {
  TestBed.configureTestingModule({
    providers: [
      provideHttpClient(),
      provideHttpClientTesting()
    ]
  });
  service = TestBed.inject(AuthenticationService);
});
```

LISTING 18-2: authentication.service.spec.ts

In the components where we use forms, the import of the Forms and ReactiveForms module will also be required:

```
beforeEach(async () => {
  await TestBed.configureTestingModule({
    declarations: [LoginComponent],
    imports: [RouterModule.forRoot([]),
      ReactiveFormsModule],
    providers: [
      provideHttpClient(),
      provideHttpClientTesting()
    ]
  })
  .compileComponents();

  fixture = TestBed.createComponent(LoginComponent);
  component = fixture.componentInstance;
  fixture.detectChanges();
});
```

LISTING 18-3: login.component.spec.ts

We also have to add imports for pagination:

```
beforeEach(async () => {
  await TestBed.configureTestingModule({
    declarations: [ItemsComponent],
    imports: [RouterModule.forRoot([]),
      FormsModule,
      NgbPagination],
    providers: [
      provideHttpClient(),
      provideHttpClientTesting()
    ]
  })
  .compileComponents();

  fixture = TestBed.createComponent(ItemsComponent);
  component = fixture.componentInstance;
  fixture.detectChanges();
});
```

LISTING 18-4: items.component.spec.ts

We will need to make the NgbActiveModal service available in the tests where a modal dialog is used (in the Filter and ErrorDialog components). This time we use the providers keyword:

```
beforeEach(async () => {
  await TestBed.configureTestingModule({
    declarations: [FilterComponent],
    imports: [RouterModule.forRoot([]),
    FormsModule],
    providers: [
      provideHttpClient(),
      provideHttpClientTesting(),
      NgbActiveModal
    ]
  })
    .compileComponents();

  fixture = TestBed.createComponent(FilterComponent);
  component = fixture.componentInstance;
  fixture.detectChanges();
});
```

LISTING 18-5: filter.component.spec.ts

Then, we should also add imports for Apollo:

```
beforeEach(async () => {
  await TestBed.configureTestingModule({
    declarations: [AdminOrdersComponent],
    imports: [RouterModule.forRoot([]),
    FormsModule,
    NgbPagination,
    ApolloTestingModule],
    providers: [
      provideHttpClient(),
      provideHttpClientTesting()
    ]
  })
    .compileComponents();

  fixture = TestBed.createComponent(AdminOrdersComponent);
  component = fixture.componentInstance;
  fixture.detectChanges();
});
```

LISTING 18-6: admin-orders.component.spec.ts

Finally, we should add imports for the reCAPTCHA modules in the registration component:

```
beforeEach(async () => {
  await TestBed.configureTestingModule({
    declarations: [RegistrationComponent],
    imports: [RouterModule.forRoot([]),
    ReactiveFormsModule,
    RecaptchaFormsModule,
    RecaptchaModule],
```

```
      providers: [
        provideHttpClient(),
        provideHttpClientTesting()
      ]
    })
    .compileComponents();

    fixture = TestBed.createComponent(RegistrationComponent);
    component = fixture.componentInstance;
    fixture.detectChanges();
  });
```

LISTING 18-7: registration.component.spec.ts

We will also remove the tests from *analytics.directive.spec.ts* so that we can make all our tests run. We will come back to it in the next chapter.

After we have made those additions to our test files, we see that all tests pass successfully. Now we are ready to add our own tests!

Testing Components

We will start with testing the `Items` component. We want to make sure that the following functionality works:

- Updating page when the number of products per page changes
- Updating page when the filter changes
- Changing pages with navigation toolbar
- Viewing a product and returning back to the same page (should preserve page number)

Let's see the first test case in full:

```
describe('ItemsComponent items per page', () => {
  let component: ItemsComponent;
  let fixture: ComponentFixture<ItemsComponent>;

  beforeEach(async () => {

    let testItems1: ItemPayload = {
      count: 14,
      items: [
        { id: 1, name: "a1", price: 1, category: "", description: "" },
        { id: 2, name: "a2", price: 1, category: "", description: "" },
        { id: 3, name: "a3", price: 1, category: "", description: "" }
      ]
    };
    let testItems2: ItemPayload = {
      count: 14,
      items: [
        { id: 1, name: "a1", price: 1, category: "", description: "" },
```

```
      { id: 2, name: "a2", price: 1, category: "", description: "" },
      { id: 3, name: "a3", price: 1, category: "", description: "" },
      { id: 4, name: "a4", price: 1, category: "", description: "" },
      { id: 5, name: "a5", price: 1, category: "", description: "" }
    ]
  };
  const itemService = jasmine.createSpyObj('ItemService', ['getItems']);
  const getItemsSpy
    = itemService.getItems.and.returnValues(of(testItems1), of(testItems2));

  await TestBed.configureTestingModule({
    declarations: [ItemsComponent],
    imports: [RouterModule.forRoot([]),
      FormsModule,
      NgbPagination],
    providers: [
      provideHttpClient(),
      provideHttpClientTesting(),
      { provide: ItemService, useValue: itemService }
    ]
  })
    .compileComponents();
});

beforeEach(() => {
  fixture = TestBed.createComponent(ItemsComponent);
  component = fixture.componentInstance;
  fixture.detectChanges();
});

it('should create', () => {
  expect(component).toBeTruthy();
});

it('should initially show 3 items', () => {
  let el = fixture.nativeElement.querySelectorAll('.card');
  expect(el.length).toEqual(3);
});

it('should show 5 items after page size change', () => {
  let el = fixture.nativeElement.querySelectorAll('.card');
  expect(el.length)
    .withContext('starting with 3 items')
    .toEqual(3);

  const select: HTMLSelectElement
    = fixture.nativeElement.querySelector('#pageSize');
  select.value = select.options[1].value;  // select a new value (5)
  select.dispatchEvent(new Event('change'));
  fixture.detectChanges();

  el = fixture.nativeElement.querySelectorAll('.card');
  expect(el.length)
    .withContext('finishing with 5 items')
    .toEqual(5);
```

```
      expect(component.storeService.page).toEqual(1);
    });
  });
```

LISTING 18-8: items.component.spec.ts

Before running the three test cases, we need to mock the `ItemService` that this component depends on. For this, we use Jasmine's `createSpyObj` function. Here, we choose to spy on `getItems` function from `ItemService`. More specifically, we give the instructions that this function will be called two times. On the first time, an array of 3 items will be returned, while on the second time there will be 5 items. This is what `ItemService` will return after we use the drop-down element to change the page size from 3 to 5 items per page.

Our tests can gain access to the component DOM with the use of the `nativeElement` property of the created component. Here, we use functions `querySelection()` and `querySelectionAll()` with CSS selectors (`#pageSize` and `.card`) to get access to the page size drop-down and the item cards respectively.

With regard to the drop-down element, we select a new value (5 items per page) and we dispatch the change event. Afterwards, we call `detectChanges()` to trigger a change detection cycle. Then, we verify that our component indeed displays 5 items on the page.

Another interesting test case is the page filter change:

```
describe('ItemsComponent filter change', () => {
  let component: ItemsComponent;
  let fixture: ComponentFixture<ItemsComponent>;

  beforeEach(async () => {
    let testItems1: ItemPayload = {
      count: 14,
      items: [
        { id: 1, name: "a1", price: 1, category: "shoes", description: "" },
        { id: 2, name: "a2", price: 1, category: "clothes", description: "" },
        { id: 3, name: "a3", price: 1, category: "shoes", description: "" }
      ]
    };
    let testItems2: ItemPayload = {
      count: 14,
      items: [
        { id: 11, name: "b1", price: 1, category: "", description: "" },
        { id: 12, name: "b2", price: 1, category: "", description: "" },
        { id: 13, name: "b3", price: 1, category: "", description: "" }
      ]
    };
    let testItems3: ItemPayload = {
      count: 5,
      items: [
        { id: 1, name: "a1", price: 1, category: "shoes", description: "" },
        { id: 3, name: "a3", price: 1, category: "shoes", description: "" },
        { id: 4, name: "a4", price: 1, category: "shoes", description: "" }
```

```
    ]
  };
  const itemService = jasmine.createSpyObj('ItemService', ['getItems']);
  let getItemsSpy
     = itemService.getItems.and.returnValues(of(testItems1),
       of(testItems2), of(testItems3));

  await TestBed.configureTestingModule({
    declarations: [ItemsComponent],
    imports: [RouterModule.forRoot([]),
      FormsModule,
      NgbPagination],
    providers: [
      provideHttpClient(),
      provideHttpClientTesting(),
      { provide: ItemService, useValue: itemService }
    ]
  })
    .compileComponents();
});

beforeEach(() => {
  fixture = TestBed.createComponent(ItemsComponent);
  component = fixture.componentInstance;
  fixture.detectChanges();
});

it('should show go to first page after filter change', () => {
  component.onPageChange(3);
  fixture.detectChanges();
  expect(component.storeService.page).toEqual(3);

  const newFilter: Filter = { name: "", categories: ["shoes"] };
  component.storeService.filter = newFilter;
  fixture.detectChanges();
  const el = fixture.nativeElement.querySelectorAll('.card');

  expect(component.storeService.page).toEqual(1);
});

});
```

LISTING 18-9: items.component.spec.ts

Here, the ItemService spy object is set to return 3 times:

- After we load the component
- After we change to page 3
- After we change the filter

We change the filter by setting the filter object in StoreService. As a result, we should check that we return to the first page as expected.

A sidenote about `StoreService`: one would expect to mock also this service, as we did with `ItemService`. However, there is no use mocking it, as it does not contain any important functionality (being a mere collection of `BehaviorSubject` objects).

Now, let's move to the `ItemDetailsComponent`. The test cases here are much simpler, but we will also see them as they include route testing functionality:

```
describe('ItemDetailsComponent', () => {
  let component: ItemDetailsComponent;
  let fixture: ComponentFixture<ItemDetailsComponent>;
  let route: ActivatedRoute;

  beforeEach(async () => {

    let testItem = {
      id: 1, name: "a1", price: 1, category: "",
      description: ""
    };
    const itemService = jasmine.createSpyObj('ItemService', ['getItem']);
    let getItemsSpy = itemService.getItem.and.returnValue(of(testItem));

    await TestBed.configureTestingModule({
      declarations: [ItemDetailsComponent],
      imports: [RouterModule.forRoot([])],
      providers: [
        provideHttpClient(),
        provideHttpClientTesting(),
        { provide: ItemService, useValue: itemService }
      ]
    })
    .compileComponents();

    fixture = TestBed.createComponent(ItemDetailsComponent);
    component = fixture.componentInstance;
    fixture.detectChanges();
  });

  beforeEach(() => {
    route = TestBed.inject(ActivatedRoute);
    spyOn(route.snapshot.paramMap, 'get').and.returnValue('1'); //itemID = 1

    fixture = TestBed.createComponent(ItemDetailsComponent);
    component = fixture.componentInstance;
    fixture.detectChanges();
  });

  it('should create', () => {
    expect(component).toBeTruthy();
  });

  it('should display selected item', () => {
    expect(component.item.name).toEqual('a1');
  });
```

```
  it('should add item to cart and navigate to cart page',
    inject([Router], (router: Router) => {
    spyOn(router, 'navigate').and.stub();

    const addToCartButton: HTMLElement
      = fixture.debugElement.query(By.css('#addToCart')).nativeElement;
    addToCartButton.dispatchEvent(new Event('click'));
    fixture.detectChanges();
    expect(component.storeService.cart.cartItems.length).toEqual(1);
    expect(router.navigate).toHaveBeenCalledWith(['/cart']);
  }));
});
```

LISTING 18-10: item.component.spec.ts

The new stuff here is Jasmine's spyOn function that we use in two places:

First of all, we use it to mock the paramMap property of the route snapshot, so that it returns the correct ID of the item to be displayed in the newly created component.

Then, we use it to mock the navigate function of the router object. Note that the actual function is not called eventually (by using: .and.stub).

In the third and more interesting case, we can see another way of getting access to the nativeElement property. We use the debugElement property of the component, which wraps the native elements of the component. A reason to use this would be that we happen to run our tests in a non-browser platform. As long as we run our tests through a browser, we are ok to access the nativeElement property directly.

At the end of the test, we can verify that the item has been inserted into the cart and that we navigate to the cart details page.

In the next article, we will continue with the unit testing scenarios. You may find the code for this chapter here:

https://github.com/htset/htset-eshop-angular-18-spring/tree/part18

19. Angular testing – part 2

In this chapter, we will continue with frontend testing. We will see how to test complex components and asynchronous operations. We will also delve into services and interceptors testing.

Testing complex components

Components may have a complex structure, with a variety of @if expressions that control how it will be rendered. Furthermore, it may contain one or more nested components.

For this demonstration we will use CheckoutComponent, as it is rather complicated, and it also contains a nested component (DeliveryAddressComponent).

First of all, we want to verify that the component is rendered correctly. The appearance of the component depends on the following:

- whether the user is logged in or not
- whether a delivery address has been already stored for this user
- whether the cart is empty or not

The following snippet depicts the case where a user has been logged in, and has already entered a delivery address in the past:

```
beforeEach(async () => {
  await TestBed.configureTestingModule({
    declarations: [CheckoutComponent, DummyChildComponent],
    imports: [RouterModule.forRoot([]),
      FormsModule],
    providers: [
      provideHttpClient(),
      provideHttpClientTesting(),
      {
        provide: AuthenticationService,
        useClass: AuthenticationServiceStub
      }
    ]
  })
    .compileComponents();
});

beforeEach(() => {
  fixture = TestBed.createComponent(CheckoutComponent);
  component = fixture.componentInstance;
  component.storeService.user = new User(); //authenticated user
  component.storeService.user.id = 1;
  component.storeService.cart.emptyCart();
});

it('should show empty cart and one address', () => {
  spyOn(component.userService, 'getAddressByUserId')
```

```
      .and.returnValue(of([testAddress1]));
    fixture.detectChanges();
    expect(fixture.debugElement.query(By.css("#cartBody")))
      .withContext('cartBody')
      .toBeNull();
    expect(fixture.debugElement.query(By.css("#noCartBody")).nativeElement)
      .withContext('noCartBody')
      .toBeTruthy();
    expect(fixture.debugElement.query(By.css("#addressBody")).nativeElement)
      .withContext('addressBody')
      .toBeTruthy();
    expect(fixture.debugElement.query(By.css("#loginLink")))
      .withContext('loginLink')
      .toBeNull();
    expect(component.storeService.deliveryAddress)
      .toEqual(-1);
    expect(fixture.debugElement
      .queryAll(By.css('input[name="selectedAddress"]')).length)
      .withContext('addresses table')
      .toEqual(2);
    expect(fixture.debugElement
      .queryAll(By.css('input[name="selectedAddress"]:checked')).length)
      .toEqual(0);
});
```

LISTING 19-1: checkout.component.spec.ts

To make those tests run, we have to create the `AuthenticationServiceStub` class in a new folder called `mocks`:

```
import { BehaviorSubject, of } from 'rxjs';
import { User } from '../models/user';

let testUser: User =
{
  id: 1,
  username: 'test',
  password: '',
  firstName: 'Test',
  lastName: 'user',
  token: '',
  role: 'admin',
  email: 'test@test.com'
};

export class AuthenticationServiceStub {

  public get currentUserValue(): User {
    let currentUserSubject: BehaviorSubject<User>
      = new BehaviorSubject<User>(testUser);
    return currentUserSubject.value;
  }
```

}

LISTING 19-2: authentication.service.mock.ts

Note that, before each test, we call the `empty()` function of the cart in order to delete the cart contents in the store service, and most importantly, in the session storage.

Testing nested components

Now, we would like to test how `CheckoutComponent` interacts with `DeliveryAddressComponent`. This component receives a predefined address as input and emits an `addresssChangedEvent` with the newly edited address as output.

We can test this interaction by creating a dymmy child component that will implement only the input and output of `DeliveryAddressComponent`:

```
@Component({ selector: 'app-delivery-address', template: '{{address}}' })
class DummyChildComponent {
  address = model<Address>();

  ngOnInit() {
    console.log('on dummy init');
    console.log(this.address);
  }
  onDummySubmit() {
    console.log('on dummy submit');
    console.log(this.address);
    this.address.set(modifiedTestAddress);
  }
}
```

LISTING 19-3: checkout.component.spec.ts

In our tests, we verify that the nested dummy component gets rendered when we select to modify an existing address. We also test whether this address is correctly refreshed upon modification in the dummy component:

```
describe('CheckoutComponent delivery address', () => {
  let component: CheckoutComponent;
  let fixture: ComponentFixture<CheckoutComponent>;

  beforeEach(async () => {
    await TestBed.configureTestingModule({
      declarations: [CheckoutComponent, DummyChildComponent],
      imports: [RouterModule.forRoot([]),
        FormsModule],
      providers: [
        provideHttpClient(),
        provideHttpClientTesting(),
        {
```

```
        provide: AuthenticationService,
        useClass: AuthenticationServiceStub
      }
    ]
  })
    .compileComponents();
});

beforeEach(() => {
  fixture = TestBed.createComponent(CheckoutComponent);
  component = fixture.componentInstance;
  component.storeService.user = new User(); //authenticated user
  component.storeService.user.id = 1;
});

it('should be editable after Modify button click', () => {
  component.storeService.cart.cartItems = [{ item: testItem, quantity: 1 }];
  spyOn(component.userService, 'getAddressByUserId')
    .and.returnValue(of([testAddress1]));
  fixture.detectChanges();
  expect(component.storeService.deliveryAddress)
    .toEqual(-1);
  expect(fixture.debugElement.nativeElement
    .querySelector('app-delivery-address'))
    .toBeNull();

  let el: HTMLButtonElement = fixture.debugElement
    .query(By.css('#modify1')).nativeElement;
  el.dispatchEvent(new Event("click"));
  fixture.detectChanges();

  console.log(fixture.debugElement
    .query(By.css('app-delivery-address')));
  console.log(fixture.debugElement.nativeElement
    .querySelector('app-delivery-address'));
  expect(fixture.debugElement.nativeElement
    .querySelector('app-delivery-address')).not.toBeNull();
});

it('should refresh address after modification', () => {
  component.storeService.cart.cartItems = [{ item: testItem, quantity: 1 }];
  let spy = spyOn(component.userService, 'getAddressByUserId')
    .and.returnValues(of([testAddress1, testAddress2]));
  fixture.detectChanges();

  expect(component.storeService.deliveryAddress)
    .toEqual(-1);
  expect(fixture.debugElement.nativeElement
    .querySelector('app-delivery-address'))
    .toBeNull();

  let el: HTMLButtonElement = fixture.debugElement
    .query(By.css('#modify1')).nativeElement;
  el.dispatchEvent(new Event("click"));
  fixture.detectChanges();
```

```
    expect(fixture.debugElement.query(By.css('#modify1')))
      .toBeNull();
    expect(fixture.debugElement.query(By.css('#cancel1')).nativeElement)
      .toBeTruthy();

    //we do NOT create the child - it is created by the host component
    //we just access it
    let childFixture = fixture.debugElement
      .query(By.directive(DummyChildComponent));
    let childComponent = childFixture.componentInstance;

    console.log(fixture.debugElement
      .query(By.directive(DummyChildComponent)));
    console.log(fixture.debugElement
      .query(By.css('app-delivery-address')));
    console.log(fixture.debugElement.nativeElement.
      querySelector('app-delivery-address'));
    expect(fixture.debugElement.nativeElement
      .querySelector('app-delivery-address')).not.toBeNull();

    //'getAddressByUserId' will be called again (now with the modified address)
    spy.and.returnValues(of([modifiedTestAddress, testAddress2]));
    let spy2 = spyOn(component.userService, 'saveAddress')
      .and.returnValues(of(modifiedTestAddress));

    childComponent.onDummySubmit();
    fixture.detectChanges();

    expect(fixture.debugElement
      .query(By.css('#addressBody form table')).nativeElement.innerHTML)
      .toContain('tt-new');
    expect(fixture.debugElement
      .query(By.css('#modify1')).nativeElement)
      .toBeTruthy();
    expect(fixture.debugElement
      .query(By.css('#cancel1')))
      .toBeNull();
  });
});
```

LISTING 19-4: checkout.component.spec.ts

Testing asynchronous operations

Another interesting test case is the following scenario (again in CheckoutComponent):

- the user has selected a delivery address
- leaves the page (e.g. goes back to the cart)
- returns to the checkout page

In this case, the delivery address ID will have already been set in the store service when the component loads for the second time:

```
it('should have radio box checked if address has already been selected before',
fakeAsync(() => {
  spyOn(component.userService, 'getAddressByUserId')
    .and.returnValue(of([testAddress1, testAddress2]));
  component.storeService.deliveryAddress = 2;
  fixture.detectChanges();
  tick();
  expect(component.storeService.deliveryAddress).toEqual(2);
  expect(fixture.debugElement
    .queryAll(By.css('input[name="selectedAddress"]')).length)
    .withContext('addresses table')
    .toEqual(3);
  expect(fixture.debugElement
    .queryAll(By.css('input[name="selectedAddress"]:checked')).length)
    .toEqual(1);
  console.log(fixture.debugElement
    .queryAll(By.css('input[name="selectedAddress"]:checked')));
}));
```

LISTING 19-5: checkout.component.spec.ts

This test case will fail, because the checked radio boxes will be 0 instead of 1. By examining the component's template, we see that we use `ngModel` to set the initial value of the radio boxes:

```
<input type="radio"
       id="selectedAddress{{addr.id}}"
       name="selectedAddress"
       [value]="addr.id"
       [ngModel]="selectedAddressId()"
       (change)="selectionChanged($any($event.target).id)"/>
```

LISTING 19-6: checkout.component.html

It turns out that `ngModel` is asynchronous, and it will take some time to update the values of the radio boxes, after changing the delivery address ID. This is why no radio box is checked at the time of the expectations checking.

We can solve this problem with the use of `fakeAsync`:

```
it('should have radio box checked if address has already been selected before',
fakeAsync(() => {
  spyOn(component.userService, 'getAddressByUserId')
    .and.returnValue(of([testAddress1, testAddress2]));
  component.storeService.deliveryAddress = 2;
  fixture.detectChanges();
  tick();
  expect(component.storeService.deliveryAddress).toEqual(2);
```

```
    expect(fixture.debugElement
      .queryAll(By.css('input[name="selectedAddress"]')).length)
      .withContext('addresses table')
      .toEqual(3);
    expect(fixture.debugElement
      .queryAll(By.css('input[name="selectedAddress"]:checked')).length)
      .toEqual(1);
    console.log(fixture.debugElement
      .queryAll(By.css('input[name="selectedAddress"]:checked')));
}));
```

LISTING 19-7: checkout.component.spec.ts

When we wrap our test function in fakeAsync we can take control of time and simulate it as we wish. By using tick() after change detection, we allow for sufficient time to pass, so that all changes have been detected before we move to the expectations.

Now that we know about testing asynchronous operations, a question: why we did not use fakeAsync also in the case of events? The answer is that dispatchEvent() evokes event handles synchronously, so there is no need for asynchronous testing.

Testing services

In this project, nearly all services are quite simple: they call the backend using HttpClient and they just return an Observable. The only case where the service contains a bit of functionality is in AuthenticationService, where the User object is stored in the session storage. Here, we will test the login process:

```
describe('AuthenticationService', () => {
  let authService: AuthenticationService;
  let storeService: StoreService;
  let httpTestingController: HttpTestingController;
  let expectedUser: User = { username: "usr", password: "passwd" };

  beforeEach(() => {
    TestBed.configureTestingModule({
      providers: [
        provideHttpClient(),
        provideHttpClientTesting()
      ]
    });
    authService = TestBed.inject(AuthenticationService);
    storeService = TestBed.inject(StoreService);
    httpTestingController = TestBed.inject(HttpTestingController);

    sessionStorage.removeItem('user');
    storeService.user = null;
  });

  it('should be created', () => {
    expect(authService).toBeTruthy();
```

```
    });

    it("should login user with correct credentials", () => {
      authService.login("usr", "passwd")
        .subscribe((user) => {
          expect(user).toEqual(expectedUser);
          expect(sessionStorage.getItem('user'))
            .toEqual(JSON.stringify(expectedUser));
          expect(storeService.user).toEqual(expectedUser);
        });

      const req = httpTestingController
        .expectOne(`${environment.apiUrl}/users/authenticate`);
      expect(req.request.method).toEqual('POST');

      req.flush(expectedUser);
    });

    it("should return error when logging in with incorrect credentials", () => {
      let expectedBadRequest = { message: "Log in failed" };
      authService.login("usr", "wrong_passwd")
        .subscribe({
          error: (e) => {
            expect(e.status).toEqual(400);
            expect(sessionStorage.getItem('user')).toBeNull();
            expect(storeService.user).toBeNull();
          }
        });

      const req = httpTestingController
        .expectOne(`${environment.apiUrl}/users/authenticate`);
      expect(req.request.method).toEqual('POST');

      req.flush(expectedBadRequest, { status: 400, statusText: 'bad request' });
    });
});
```

LISTING 19-8: authentication.service.spec.ts

For the tests, we use the `HttpTestingController`. We inject the `AuthenticationService` object and we use it to call `login()` function and test our expectations. We mock the HTTP response so that it contains the appropriate results.

Testing interceptors

The process of interceptor testing resembles that of service testing. Here we will see how to test the interceptor that adds a token in every outgoing request to the backend (*jwt.interceptor.ts*).

During test setup, we have to provide the interceptor to the testing module. We also inject the `ItemService`, as we will use it to make authenticated requests to the API:

```
describe('HttpInterceptorService', () => {
  let itemService: ItemService;
  let storeService: StoreService;
  let httpTestingController: HttpTestingController;

  beforeEach(() => {
    TestBed.configureTestingModule({
      imports: [HttpClientTestingModule],
      providers: [
        { provide: HTTP_INTERCEPTORS, useClass: JwtInterceptor, multi: true },
      ]
    });
    itemService = TestBed.inject(ItemService);
    storeService = TestBed.inject(StoreService);
    httpTestingController = TestBed.inject(HttpTestingController);
  });

  it('should insert token for logged in users', () => {
    let testItem = {
      id: 1, name: "a1", price: 1,
      category: "", description: ""
    };
    storeService.user = new User();
    storeService.user.token = "test_token";

    itemService.getItem(1)
      .subscribe();

    const req = httpTestingController.expectOne(r =>
      r.headers.has('Authorization')
        && r.headers.get('Authorization') === 'Bearer test_token');

    req.flush(testItem);
  });

  it('should not insert token for non-logged in users', () => {
    let testItem = {
      id: 1, name: "a1", price: 1,
      category: "", description: ""
    };
    storeService.user = null;

    itemService.getItem(1)
      .subscribe();

    const req = httpTestingController.expectOne(r =>
      !r.headers.has('Authorization'));

    req.flush(testItem);
  });
})
```

LISTING 19-9: jwt.interceptor.spec.ts

In both test cases, we check whether the request headers contain the token or not.

Directives testing

Finally, we will see how to test our directive. We will create a test component and will apply the directive to this:

```
@Component({
  template: `<input type="button"
             id="test" value="Test"
             appAnalytics events="click" />`
})
class TestComponent {
}

describe('AnalyticsDirective', () => {
  let component: TestComponent;
  let fixture: ComponentFixture<TestComponent>;
  let originalLog: any;

  beforeEach(async () => {
    await TestBed.configureTestingModule({
      declarations: [AnalyticsDirective
        , TestComponent],
    })
      .compileComponents();

    fixture = TestBed.createComponent(TestComponent);
    component = fixture.componentInstance;
    fixture.detectChanges();

    originalLog = console.log;
    spyOn(console, 'log');
  });

  afterEach(() => {
    // Restore the original console.log after each test
    console.log = originalLog;
  });

  it('should create an instance', () => {
    let el: HTMLButtonElement = fixture.debugElement
      .query(By.css('#test')).nativeElement;
    el.dispatchEvent(new Event("click"));
    fixture.detectChanges();

    expect(console.log).toHaveBeenCalled();
    expect(console.log).toHaveBeenCalledWith("Event: click");
  });
});
```

LISTING 19-10: analytics.directive.spec.ts

You can find more test cases about other components, such as CartComponent, DeliveryAddressComponent and ItemService in the code here:

https://github.com/htset/htset-eshop-angular-18-spring/tree/part19

20. Spring Boot Web API testing

We will conclude this book with some unit testing on the backend side. We will test the `ItemController` and `ItemService` classes, as they are representative of the API functionality.

When we created the Spring Boot project, we already included a dependency for testing:

```xml
<dependency>
  <groupId>org.springframework.boot</groupId>
  <artifactId>spring-boot-starter-test</artifactId>
  <scope>test</scope>
</dependency>
```

LISTING 20-1: pom.xml

Let's start with testing the `ItemService` class. `ItemService` uses `ItemRepository` to fetch data from the database. In unit testing, we test each class in isolation, and we mock all external dependencies using Mockito.

We will create a new class, `ItemServiceTest`, in package `com.example.Eshop.services` in *the tests folder*:

```java
package com.example.Eshop.services;

import com.example.Eshop.dtos.ItemPayloadDTO;
import com.example.Eshop.exceptions.ItemNotFoundException;
import com.example.Eshop.models.Item;
import com.example.Eshop.repositories.ItemRepository;
import org.junit.jupiter.api.BeforeEach;
import org.junit.jupiter.api.Test;
import org.mockito.InjectMocks;
import org.mockito.Mock;
import org.mockito.MockitoAnnotations;
import org.springframework.data.domain.Page;
import org.springframework.data.domain.PageImpl;
import org.springframework.data.domain.PageRequest;
import java.util.Arrays;
import java.util.List;
import java.util.Optional;
import static org.junit.jupiter.api.Assertions.*;
import static org.mockito.Mockito.*;

class ItemServiceTest {

  @Mock
  private ItemRepository itemRepository;

  @InjectMocks
  private ItemService itemService;

  @BeforeEach
  void setUp() {
```

```java
    MockitoAnnotations.openMocks(this);
  }

  @Test
  void testGetItems_Success() {
    int page = 1;
    int size = 10;
    String category = "Clothes";
    String name = "Nike sweater";

    List<Item> items = Arrays.asList(new Item(), new Item());
    Page<Item> itemPage = new PageImpl<>(items, PageRequest
        .of(page - 1, size), items.size());

    when(itemRepository
        .findByColumnContainingValuesAndFilter(anyList(),
            eq(name), any(PageRequest.class)))
        .thenReturn(itemPage);

    ItemPayloadDTO result = itemService.getItems(page, size, category, name);

    assertEquals(items.size(), result.getItems().size());
    assertEquals(items.size(), result.getCount());
  }
}
```

LISTING 20-2: ItemServiceTest.java

First, we create a mock of the `ItemRepository` class and we inject it to the test class. In the `testGetItems_Success()` method, we first initialize the parameters for pagination and search and then we create a list of `Item` objects representing the items to be returned. Then we define how `ItemRepository` should behave when its

`findByColumnContainingValuesAndFilter()`

method is called.

Afterwards, the `getItems` method of `ItemService` is called with the specified parameters. The test checks that the returned `ItemPayloadDTO` contains the correct number of items.

In order to run the test, we can right click on the Java class and select Run or Debug. We can also right click on the tests folder to run all the available tests.

Here are the complete tests for `ItemService`:

```java
package com.example.Eshop.services;

import com.example.Eshop.dtos.ItemPayloadDTO;
import com.example.Eshop.exceptions.ItemNotFoundException;
import com.example.Eshop.models.Item;
import com.example.Eshop.repositories.ItemRepository;
import org.junit.jupiter.api.BeforeEach;
import org.junit.jupiter.api.Test;
```

```java
import org.mockito.InjectMocks;
import org.mockito.Mock;
import org.mockito.MockitoAnnotations;
import org.springframework.data.domain.Page;
import org.springframework.data.domain.PageImpl;
import org.springframework.data.domain.PageRequest;
import java.util.Arrays;
import java.util.List;
import java.util.Optional;
import static org.junit.jupiter.api.Assertions.*;
import static org.mockito.Mockito.*;

class ItemServiceTest {

  @Mock
  private ItemRepository itemRepository;

  @InjectMocks
  private ItemService itemService;

  @BeforeEach
  void setUp() {
    MockitoAnnotations.openMocks(this);
  }

  @Test
  void testGetItems_Success() {
    int page = 1;
    int size = 10;
    String category = "Clothes";
    String name = "Nike sweater";

    List<Item> items = Arrays.asList(new Item(), new Item());
    Page<Item> itemPage = new PageImpl<>(items, PageRequest
        .of(page - 1, size), items.size());

    when(itemRepository
        .findByColumnContainingValuesAndFilter(anyList(),
            eq(name), any(PageRequest.class)))
        .thenReturn(itemPage);

    ItemPayloadDTO result = itemService.getItems(page, size, category, name);

    assertEquals(items.size(), result.getItems().size());
    assertEquals(items.size(), result.getCount());
  }

  @Test
  void testGetItems_InvalidPageParameters() {
    assertThrows(RuntimeException.class, () -> {
      itemService.getItems(0, 10, null, null);
    });
  }

  @Test
```

```java
void testGetItems_InternalServerError() {
    int page = 1;
    int size = 10;
    when(itemRepository.findAll(any(PageRequest.class)))
        .thenThrow(new RuntimeException("Unexpected error"));

    assertThrows(RuntimeException.class, () -> {
        itemService.getItems(page, size, null, null);
    });
}

@Test
void testGetItemById_Success() {
    Long id = 1L;
    Item item = new Item();
    item.setId(id);
    when(itemRepository.findById(id))
        .thenReturn(Optional.of(item));

    Item result = itemService.getItemById(id);

    assertEquals(item, result);
}

@Test
void testGetItemById_NotFound() {
    Long id = 1L;
    when(itemRepository.findById(id))
        .thenReturn(Optional.empty());

    assertThrows(ItemNotFoundException.class, () -> {
        itemService.getItemById(id);
    });
}

@Test
void testCreateItem_Success() {
    Item item = new Item();
    when(itemRepository.save(item)).thenReturn(item);

    Item result = itemService.createItem(item);

    assertEquals(item, result);
}

@Test
void testCreateItem_InternalServerError() {
    Item item = new Item();
    when(itemRepository.save(item))
        .thenThrow(new RuntimeException("Unexpected error"));

    assertThrows(RuntimeException.class, () -> {
        itemService.createItem(item);
    });
}
```

```java
@Test
void testUpdateItem_Success() {
  Long id = 1L;
  Item existingItem = new Item();
  existingItem.setId(id);
  existingItem.setName("Old Name");

  Item updatedItem = new Item();
  updatedItem.setName("New Name");

  when(itemRepository.findById(id))
      .thenReturn(Optional.of(existingItem));
  when(itemRepository.save(existingItem))
      .thenReturn(existingItem);

  Item result = itemService.updateItem(id, updatedItem);

  assertEquals("New Name", result.getName());
}

@Test
void testUpdateItem_NotFound() {
  Long id = 1L;
  Item updatedItem = new Item();
  when(itemRepository.findById(id))
      .thenReturn(Optional.empty());

  assertThrows(ItemNotFoundException.class, () -> {
    itemService.updateItem(id, updatedItem);
  });
}

@Test
void testDeleteItem_Success() {
  Long id = 1L;
  Item item = new Item();
  when(itemRepository.findById(id))
      .thenReturn(Optional.of(item));
  doNothing().when(itemRepository).delete(item);

  itemService.deleteItem(id);

  verify(itemRepository, times(1)).delete(item);
}

@Test
void testDeleteItem_NotFound() {
  Long id = 1L;
  when(itemRepository.findById(id))
      .thenReturn(Optional.empty());

  assertThrows(ItemNotFoundException.class, () -> {
    itemService.deleteItem(id);
  });
```

        }
}

LISTING 20-3: ItemServiceTest.java

Next, we proceed with testing the `ItemController` class. Here, we mock the `ItemService` class:

```
package com.example.Eshop.controllers;

import com.example.Eshop.dtos.ItemPayloadDTO;
import com.example.Eshop.models.Item;
import com.example.Eshop.services.ItemService;
import com.example.Eshop.exceptions.ItemNotFoundException;
import org.junit.jupiter.api.BeforeEach;
import org.junit.jupiter.api.Test;
import org.mockito.InjectMocks;
import org.mockito.Mock;
import org.mockito.MockitoAnnotations;
import org.springframework.http.HttpStatus;
import org.springframework.http.ResponseEntity;
import static org.junit.jupiter.api.Assertions.assertEquals;
import static org.mockito.Mockito.*;

class ItemControllerTest {

  @Mock
  private ItemService itemService;

  @InjectMocks
  private ItemController itemController;

  @BeforeEach
  void setUp() {
    MockitoAnnotations.openMocks(this);
  }

  @Test
  void testGetItems_Success() {
    int pageNumber = 1;
    int pageSize = 10;
    String category = "Clothes";
    String name = "Nike sweater";
    ItemPayloadDTO itemPayloadDTO = new ItemPayloadDTO();

    when(itemService.getItems(pageNumber, pageSize, category, name))
        .thenReturn(itemPayloadDTO);

    ResponseEntity<ItemPayloadDTO> response
        = itemController.getItems(pageNumber, pageSize, category, name);

    assertEquals(HttpStatus.OK, response.getStatusCode());
```

```java
    assertEquals(itemPayloadDTO, response.getBody());
}

@Test
void testGetItems_InvalidPageParameters() {
    ResponseEntity<ItemPayloadDTO> response
        = itemController.getItems(0, 10, null, null);

    assertEquals(HttpStatus.BAD_REQUEST, response.getStatusCode());
    assertEquals(null, response.getBody());
}

@Test
void testGetItems_InternalServerError() {
    int pageNumber = 1;
    int pageSize = 10;
    when(itemService.getItems(pageNumber, pageSize, null, null))
        .thenThrow(new RuntimeException("Unexpected error"));

    ResponseEntity<ItemPayloadDTO> response
        = itemController.getItems(pageNumber, pageSize, null, null);

    assertEquals(HttpStatus.INTERNAL_SERVER_ERROR, response.getStatusCode());
    assertEquals(null, response.getBody());
}

@Test
void testGetItemById_Success() {
    Long id = 1L;
    Item item = new Item();
    item.setId(id);
    when(itemService.getItemById(id)).thenReturn(item);

    ResponseEntity<Item> response = itemController.getItemById(id);

    assertEquals(HttpStatus.OK, response.getStatusCode());
    assertEquals(item, response.getBody());
}

@Test
void testGetItemById_NotFound() {
    Long id = 1L;
    when(itemService.getItemById(id))
        .thenThrow(new ItemNotFoundException("Item not found"));

    ResponseEntity<Item> response = itemController.getItemById(id);

    assertEquals(HttpStatus.NOT_FOUND, response.getStatusCode());
    assertEquals(null, response.getBody());
}

@Test
void testCreateItem_Success() {
    Item item = new Item();
    item.setName("New Item");
```

```java
    Item createdItem = new Item();
    createdItem.setId(1L);
    createdItem.setName("New Item");

    when(itemService.createItem(item)).thenReturn(createdItem);

    ResponseEntity<Item> response = itemController.createItem(item);

    assertEquals(HttpStatus.CREATED, response.getStatusCode());
    assertEquals(createdItem, response.getBody());
}

@Test
void testCreateItem_InternalServerError() {
    Item item = new Item();
    when(itemService.createItem(item))
        .thenThrow(new RuntimeException("Unexpected error"));

    ResponseEntity<Item> response
        = itemController.createItem(item);

    assertEquals(HttpStatus.INTERNAL_SERVER_ERROR,
        response.getStatusCode());
    assertEquals(null, response.getBody());
}

@Test
void testUpdateItem_Success() {
    Long id = 1L;
    Item updatedItem = new Item();
    updatedItem.setName("Updated Item");
    Item returnedItem = new Item();
    returnedItem.setId(id);
    returnedItem.setName("Updated Item");

    when(itemService.updateItem(id, updatedItem))
        .thenReturn(returnedItem);

    ResponseEntity<Item> response
        = itemController.updateItem(id, updatedItem);

    assertEquals(HttpStatus.OK, response.getStatusCode());
    assertEquals(returnedItem, response.getBody());
}

@Test
void testUpdateItem_NotFound() {
    Long id = 1L;
    Item updatedItem = new Item();
    when(itemService.updateItem(id, updatedItem))
        .thenThrow(new ItemNotFoundException("Item not found"));

    ResponseEntity<Item> response = itemController.updateItem(id, updatedItem);

    assertEquals(HttpStatus.NOT_FOUND, response.getStatusCode());
```

```
    assertEquals(null, response.getBody());
  }

  @Test
  void testDeleteItem_Success() {
    Long id = 1L;
    doNothing().when(itemService).deleteItem(id);

    ResponseEntity<Void> response
        = itemController.deleteItem(id);

    assertEquals(HttpStatus.NO_CONTENT,
        response.getStatusCode());
  }

  @Test
  void testDeleteItem_NotFound() {
    Long id = 1L;
    doThrow(new ItemNotFoundException("Item not found"))
        .when(itemService).deleteItem(id);

    ResponseEntity<Void> response
        = itemController.deleteItem(id);

    assertEquals(HttpStatus.NOT_FOUND,
        response.getStatusCode());
  }
}
```

LISTING 20-4: ItemControllerTest.java

Let's examine the first method. First, it initializes the parameters for the request and then sets up `ItemService` to return the mock data when the `getItems()` method is called with the specified parameters.

Afterwards, the `getItems()` method of `ItemController` is called and then the test checks that the response status and body are as expected.

You may find the code for this chapter here:

https://github.com/htset/htset-eshop-angular-18-spring/tree/part20

www.ingramcontent.com/pod-product-compliance
Lightning Source LLC
Chambersburg PA
CBHW062101220526
45471CB00010B/3559